# Ritual Ablutions for Women

# (Ṭahãratu 'n-Nisã')

*A comprehensive book
on the sharī'ah laws pertaining to
the ritual ablutions for women according to
the Shi'i (Ja'fari) school of jurisprudence (fiqh).*

## Sayyid Muhammad Rizvi

Al-Ma'ãrif Publications
CANADA

**1445 / 2024**

First Edition - Shawwal 1405 / June 1985
Second Edition - Rabi II 1407 / December 1986
**Third Edition - Ramadhãn 1445 / March 2024**



Rizvi, Sayyid Muhammad, 1957-
Ritual Ablutions for Women (Ṭahãratu 'n-nisã')

ISBN: 978-0-920675-21-2
e-ISBN: 978-1-990774-54-6

Published by

Al-Ma'ãrif Publications
Canada

www.al-m.ca  |  +1 (416) 624-7861  |  publications@al-m.ca

# Table of Contents

بسم الله الرحمن الرحيم
الحمد لله رب العالمين
و صل الله على محمد و آله الطاهرين

# <u>Preface of the 3rd Edition</u>

*The Ritual Ablutions for Women (Ṭahãratu 'n-Nisã')* was first published in 1985 and again in 1986. In the 90's it also became available online on al-islam.org, a free online Shī‘a resource. Shī‘a women of the English speaking world found this work to be reader-friendly and clear in describing the rulings of purity regarding their monthly cycle. After reading the first edition, one reader in Canada wrote: "Until now, I had to search in a deep ocean to find the solutions I needed...I had the greatest satisfaction in going through all the chapters and I am sure all my Muslim sisters would have the same view." Dr. Abul Hasan, from U.P., India, wrote: "The fact is that I have not seen any book, even in Urdu, with such a clarity on the subject, as you have dealt with in *Ṭahãratu 'n-Nisã'*."

Thirty six years later there is still a strong demand for this book, and so I decided to revise it in order to further clarify and simplify the rulings, as well as to update the verdicts of the senior-most living jurists *(mujtahideen)* of our time. The previous edition was based on the verdicts of the late Grand Āyatullāh Sayyid Abul Qāsim al-Khū'ī.

In this edition, I have added the views of the senior living *marãji'*, in particular the Grand Āyatullāh Sayyid 'Ali as-Sistāni.

All sections have been updated based on new rulings, frequently asked questions, and the over 170 queries submitted to us via our Al-Ma'ãrif website (al-m.ca) when we solicited questions from the public while preparing this latest edition. We would like to thank those who anonymously contributed towards the usefulness of this book through their questions.

Revising this book had been in the pipeline for the last few years but it probably wouldn't have materialized now if it wasn't for the constant encouragement & support of my wife, and those who would approach her with new questions and situations.

Once again, I thank Almighty Allãh for giving me an opportunity to serve His chosen religion, and may He accept this humble work from one of His most humble servants.

<table>
<tr><td>Toronto, ON</td><td>Sayyid Muhammad Rizvi</td></tr>
<tr><td>Canada</td><td>publications@al-m.ca</td></tr>
<tr><td>Ramadhãn 1445 / March 2024</td><td></td></tr>
</table>

بسم الله الرحمن الرحيم
الحمد لله رب العالمين
و صلى الله على محمد و آله الطاهرين

## <u>Abstract from the Preface of the 1st Edition</u>

Knowing laws regarding monthly periods and pre- or post-natal bleeding is an essential duty of every Muslim woman. But the unavailability of a comprehensive book in English on this subject has made access to these laws almost impossible for those Muslim women who are unfamiliar with Arabic, Persian or Urdu. One reason for the unavailability of such a book in English is that in many Muslim communities, open discussion of this and similar subjects are taboo. This, plus the complexity of the laws of menstruation (which arises from the vast differences in the patterns of women's menstrual cycles) may have discouraged many writers from dealing with this subject comprehensively.

The present writer, by putting his trust in Almighty Allāh, has tried to accomplish this task and has simplified, to his utmost ability, the laws of the *sharī'ah* regarding women and their monthly periods.

In the end, I thank Almighty Allāh for giving me an opportunity to serve His chosen religion, and may He accept this humble work from one of His most humble servants.

Richmond, B.C.                                    S. M. Rizvi
Ramadhān 1405
May 1985

# How To Read This Book

This book consists of three sections:
1. Menstruation
2. Irregular Bleeding
3. Childbirth Bleeding

Sections 2 and 3 are to be read normally. However for Section 1, the following instructions will provide clarity to the reader, and will help her avoid confusion.

There are 3 stages for reading the first part of this book on menstruation:

**Firstly**, you are advised to read the first four chapters that cover the introduction, definition of a cycle, age categories, and signs, duration, and categories of cycles.
In the fourth chapter, you will find the definitions of different categories of women in their monthly periods. You will use this to identify the appropriate category which applies to you.

**Secondly**, proceed to read <u>only</u> one of the next four chapters (5-8) which is <u>applicable to you</u>. Avoid reading other categories in order to minimize any potential confusion between the different rulings.

**Thirdly**, read the last four chapters (chaps. 9-12) regarding general rules for everyday life.

Regarding regular periods in chapter six, I have

provided some charts to simplify and visualize the laws. To understand the chart, please observe the following example:

*The numbers in the top row represent specific days of a month.*

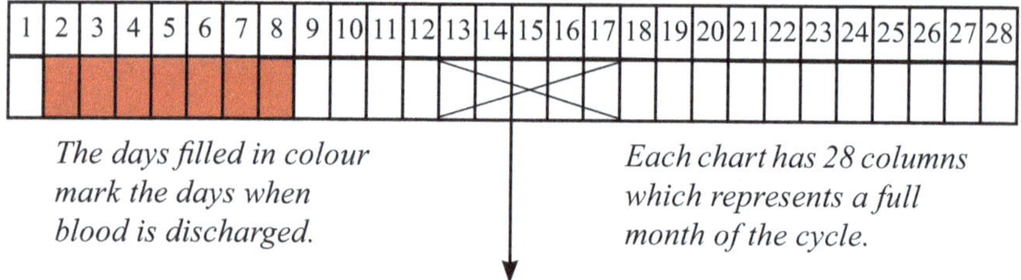

*The days filled in colour mark the days when blood is discharged.*

*Each chart has 28 columns which represents a full month of the cycle.*

*The cross within the boxes indicates the fixed time and number of days of a woman's period.*

Towards the end, a calender has been provided to help you keep track of your monthly cycle. More resources can be found at https://al-m.ca/nisa.

# <u>Part One</u>

# The Laws of Menstruation

## 1. Introduction

Menstruation is a natural process which takes place in a female's body every month.

Before explaining the Islamic laws regarding menstruation, it seems appropriate to discuss why this process takes place.

Almighty Allãh has created the woman such that she plays a major role in the perpetuation of the human race. The primary reproductive organs of a woman are her ovaries. When a girl is born, her ovaries already contain about 400,000 immature eggs (which are known as ova). At puberty, the eggs start maturing, usually one ovum each month. The maturing of the ovum takes place roughly halfway between two menstrual cycles. After maturing, it finds its way from the ovary to the fallopian tube and ends up in the womb. Meanwhile, the womb (while preparing for the possible arrival of a fertilized egg) develops a thick, soft, velvet-like lining which is made up mostly of blood vessels. This thick, soft lining in the womb is called the endometrium. If an egg is fertilized, it will be embedded in the endometrium and continues its growth. However if no egg is fertilized, the endometrium (i.e. the lining of the womb) is no longer needed and is shed or discarded. This process of discarding the endometrium is known as menstruation.

From this biological explanation, menstruation is neither a "curse" on women, nor is it a result of the so-called "original sin of Eve"; rather it is a very normal biological process that ensures the perpetuation of the human race.

Some girls and women experience painful cramps before and during menstruation. This discomfort is caused by the biological changes taking place in a female's body. Almighty Allāh says, *"They ask you about menstruation. (O Muḥammad), 'tell them that menstruation is a discomfort for the women'"* (2:222). It causes physical discomfort, and at times, emotional fluctuation.

In this book I intend, by putting my trust in Almighty Allāh, to explain the Islamic laws regarding women who are in their monthly periods. First, the definition of menstruation, its signs, and its duration will be discussed. Then comes the different categories of women who are in menstruation; followed by four chapters on the laws regarding women in each of those specific categories. Finally, the acts which are forbidden to a woman during her periods, and the manner of *ghusl* are explained.

## 2. Defining a Monthly Cycle *(Ḥayz)*

There are four possible causes for a discharge of blood from women:
1. Menstruation
2. Loss of virginity
3. Childbirth and postpartum bleeding
4. Internal injury

The first cause, **menstruation**, is different from the blood caused by the other 3 categories. In Islamic legal terminology, menstruation is known as *hayz*, and a woman who is having her period is known as *hã'iz*.[1]

Regarding the second cause, if a woman loses her **virginity**, and so much blood is discharged that she is uncertain whether the blood is from the loss of virginity or menstruation or both, then she should examine herself "by inserting a piece of cotton inside her vagina and leave it there for a while. Then she should take it out gently – if the blood has only stained the outside of the cotton, then it is from the loss of virginity; but if the blood has penetrated into the cotton, then it is menstruation."[2] In the context of present-day, cotton can be replaced with a folded piece of bathroom tissue, to be placed inside for a minute or so.

## Beginning Age:

According to Islamic laws, menstruation is the process of discarding the endometrium. This normally takes place approximately once a month in women from the age of puberty until they reach the age of menopause (the final cessation of menstruation.)[3].

From the *sharī'ah* point of view, a girl attains **puberty** at the completion of her **nine lunar years**, i.e., at the 9th lunar birthday which, according to the common calendar, would be at **eight years, nine months and twenty days**.

---

1     To simplfy the pronunciation, I have departed from the standard transliteration of writing ض as "ḍ" and ذ as "dh," and instead I have used "z" in both cases. And so instead of *hã'iḍ* and *hayḍ,* I have written *hã'iz* and *hayz;* and instead of *dhãt,* I have simply used *zãt.*

2     As explained by Imãm Mūsa al-Kãzim (a.s.) to Khalaf bin Ḥammãd al-Kūfī. See al-ʿÃmilī, *Wasã'ilu 'sh-Shī'ah,* vol. 2, p. 535.

3     Qur'ãn 4:64 talks about both types of women, "those who have menstruation" as well as "those who cease to have menstruation."

So, if a girl sees blood **before** her ninth lunar birthday, that blood is not considered menstruation, *even if* it may be regarded as menstruation from the medical point of view.

If the three signs of *ḥayz*, which are described later in this chapter, create certainty, then it will be an indication that she has become nine years.[1]

## Ending Age:

According to the *sharī'ah,* a lady reaches the age of **menopause** at her **fiftieth lunar year**. Imãm Ja'far aṣ-Ṣādiq (a.s.) said, "The age when a woman ceases to have menstruation is fifty years."[2] Fifty lunar years, according to the common calendar, would be **forty-eight years, six months and four days.**

**Sãdãt women:** For sãdãt women, the beginning of menopause is at the age of sixty of the lunar calendar which, according to the common calendar, would be **fifty-nine years, two months and sixteen days.**

In the same way, if a woman sees blood **after** the age of fifty that blood will not be considered menstruation.

If a woman who **doubts** whether or not she has reached the age of menopause, sees blood, then she should consider it as menstruation.

## Menopause:

If a woman who has already reached the age of menopause (i.e., fifty lunar years) sees blood on herself with the three signs of menstruation present, or at the fixed time of her monthly periods, then she will consider it as

---

1    Khū'ī: If a girl **does not know** if she has become nine years old and she sees blood, then it's not considered menstruation even if it has all three signs of *ḥayz*.

2    Al-Ḥurr al-'Ãmili, *op. cit.,* vol. 2, p. 580.

*ḥayz*; however, it is better *(iḥtiyāṭ mustaḥab)* for her to act on precaution up to the age of sixty.[1]

**"Act on precaution"** in the above context, means to refrain from those things which are forbidden to a *ḥā'iz* and perform those things which are required of a woman in *istiḥāzah*. (*Istiḥāzah* is defined as 'irregular patterns', which will be discussed later in this book.)

**Sādāt women:** This rule of "acting on precaution" from age 50 to 60 (of lunar years) does not apply to sādāt; for them, the beginning of menopause is at the age of sixty of the lunar calendar which, according to the common calendar, would be **fifty-nine years, two months and sixteen days.**

**Pre-menopause:** When the monthly pattern duration starts to constantly change, then you should examine yourself for the signs covered later in this chapter. If you see that you are clean, then you should consider youself as pure and perform *ghuslu 'l-ḥayz*. If you are unable to examine yourself, then you should consider it as *ḥayz* until you are sure of your purity.

Any blood seen after the age of sixty will not be considered *ḥayz*.

*****

**In summary**, if there is blood discharge...

| | |
|---|---|
| Before age 9 | - no specific duty |
| Between age 9 to 50 | - *ḥayz* |
| Between age 50 to 60 | - refer to 'Menopause' section |
| After 60+ | - *istiḥāzah* |

---

1  Khū'ī: She **must** act on precaution, based on *iḥtiyāṭ wājib,* up to the age of sixty. However, since this view is based on *iḥtiyāṭ,* she can refer to Sistāni whose ruling is that she should consider it as *ḥayz*.

Additionally, according to the *sharī'ah*, it is possible for a pregnant woman and a nursing mother to have menstruation. These topics are covered in later chapters.

*****

The new terms introduced in the past few pages, that will be used throughout the book, include:

| | |
|---|---|
| *ḥãyz* | - menstruation |
| *ḥã'iz* | - a woman in menstruation |
| *istiḥãzah* | - irregular pattern |
| *iḥtiyãṭ wãjib* | - wãjib based on precaution |

## The Signs of *Ḥayz*:

If a woman is not sure about the nature of her discharge, then she should look for the following three signs of menstrual blood:

1. warmth
2. bright red to dark brown or black colour
3. pressure and slight burning in the discharge

If these three signs are found **together**, and it is only observed **outside** the vagina, not inside it, then it is considered as menstruation.

These signs have been taken from a *hadīth* of Imãm Ja'far aṣ-Ṣãdiq (a). A woman came to him and asked, "What should a woman do who sees blood on herself but does not know whether it is menstruation or some other type (of blood)?"

The Imãm said, "The blood of menstruation is warm... black (or dark-coloured), and it has pressure and burning sensation..." The woman said, "By Allãh! If he had been a woman, he could not have added anything further in this (description)!"[1]

## Doubts in the Signs of *Ḥayz*:

There are various situations where a woman may be unsure of what they've observed when checking themselves. This section will attempt to address these scenarios.

If there is a discharge of varying type and thickness, and it has all three signs for at least three days and less than ten days, then it is considered to be menses.

If a woman with regular monthly cycles experiences unusual mid-cycle bleeding from the cervix or other source, and is sure it isn't menstrual, she should consider it as *istiḥāzah*.

Continuous flow is a sign of *ḥayz*. However, if a woman regularly experiences spotting as her natural cycle, or due to a medical condition, this will be considered to be her regular pattern and *ḥayz*, if it continues for three or more days.

If during every cycle a woman is regularly spotting for a day or less than a day, and it is coupled with pain, it will be considered the beginning of *ḥayz*, even if the three signs are not present.

Vaginal discharge as a result of a yeast infection is not considered najis, nor is it considered *ḥayz*.

---

1    Ibid., p. 537.

If a white or clear secretion is discharged from a woman without sexual passion or a feeling of relaxation after it, then it is not najis and so no *ghusl* is required, and it is not considered *ḥayz*.

## Birth Control & the Signs of *Ḥayz*:

Most birth control pill routines include some days at the end of a month where a period is to occur. However some women only experience spotting for a few days. If this happens every month, it will be considered your regular monthly cycle. However if it occurs for less than 3 days, it will be considered *istiḥāzah*.

# 3. Duration of *Ḥayz*

The beginning of menstruation is determined to be when blood leaves the uterus and enters the vagina. However, the rules of *ḥayz* commence only when the blood is seen outside the vagina.

In another *ḥadīth*, Imām aṣ-Ṣādiq (a) said, "The **minimum** duration of menstruation is **three days**, and the **maximum** is **ten days**."[1]

"**Three days**" means three continuous days and the two nights in between. "Continuous" does not mean that it's constantly flowing, rather a woman should 'feel' it for the three days. So, if a woman sees blood for less than three days, it is not considered *ḥayz*.

For example, if blood starts on Monday morning and stops on Wednesday evening, then it is menstruation.

---

1    Ibid., p. 551.

"**Ten days**" means ten days and the nine nights between the first and the tenth day.

If blood is seen for more than ten days, the ten days will be counted as menstruation and the blood seen after that will be regarded as _istiḥāzah_ (irregular bleeding).

The same Imām said, "The minimum duration of purity (between two menstrual cycles) must be (at least) ten days."[1] So if a woman sees blood during the ten days after her period had ended, it will not be considered _ḥayz_.

**In summary:**
minimum duration of _ḥayz_: 3 days
maximum duration of _ḥayz_: 10 days
minimum purity between two cycles: 10 days

It is generally said that menstruation takes place once "a month," but it should be clarified that menstrual cycles take place every 28 days—so, in the present context "a month" means a duration of 28 days, not 29, 30 or 31 days.

You should perform _ghusl_ as soon as _ḥayz_ has ended, and not postpone it. This is covered in later chapters.

Period tracking mobile apps can be used to help log the duration. While they cannot be used to exactly predict when your cycle starts and ends, they are a good tool to roughly estimate, and there is no issue with using them.

---

1    Ibid., p. 554.

## Doubts of Duration:

There are situations where a woman may have doubts regarding the duration of her cycle. This section will attempt to address those scenarios.

Any spotting observed after your **regular** pattern has passed, is to be considered *istiḥāzah*, not menses. If you have an **irregular** pattern, your situation will be covered later in this book.

If a woman with an **irregular** pattern sees blood and does not know whether or not it will last for three days, then she should cease praying and fasting. If it ends before 3 days, she should perform *qazā* of those rituals. If the blood stops after 3 days but before 10 days, then she should examine herself; if there is no blood, then she should consider herself pure and perform the *ghusl* of *ḥayz*.

If a woman has a **regular** pattern and sees 1-2 drops of discharge, and then nothing for 24 hours, and then a continuous flow afterwards, then the early discharge is considered *istiḥāzah* and the continuous flow is considered *ḥayz*. If you have an **irregular** pattern and observe a similar situation, then it is addressed further in the book.

If a discharge of 2 to 4 days before the actual period also occured with warmth and pressure, and together with the 'actual' period was between three to ten days, then the entire duration of discharge will be considered as *ḥayz*.

If there is an abnormal pause in the flow before your usual cycle ends, and you know it usually continues after the pause then you should still consider yourself *ḥā'iz* during the pause. If you consider yourself *ḥā'iz* during the pause and the flow does not return, then consider your menstruation as complete, and you will have to perform *qazā ṣalāt* or fasts of those missed days. There should be no guilt felt for missing out on those rituals in such a situation.

If in a 5 day cycle, you see a flow for the first two days and then very light spotting for the next three days, and your regular cycle is normally 5 days, then you will consider all 5 days as *ḥayz*.

If a woman experiences spotting for multiple weeks **externally**, and she experiences regular patterns, then consider those fixed days as *ḥayz* and the rest as *istiḥāzah*.

## Birth Control & the Duration of *Ḥayz*:

Most birth control pill routines include some days at the end of a month where a period is to occur.

If a woman with regular cycles who is on birth control pills and experiences spotting at same time as her menses usually occured in the past, and it continues for 3 days, it will be considered *ḥayz*; otherwise, it is *istiḥāzah*.

However some women skip these pills and continue straight to the next active pill cycle, in order to avoid having a period. This may be done for Ramadhān to be able to fast, or for travels such as *ziyārat*, *hajj*, *'umrah* etc. Occasionally this results in light bleeding or spotting. If this occurs at the time of your regular cycle, it will be considered *ḥayz*, as in the skipping of a period was not successful. However if it occurs for less than 3 days, it will be considered *istiḥāzah*.

If you have been regularly skipping these pills and don't know or have regular cycles, then count the number of days it occurs: if less than 3 days, it is *istiḥãzah*, and if more than 3, it is *ḥayz*.

If a woman in the above scenario takes the pill to avoid a period even if they don't expect it to start, and still experiences spotting outside of their fixed days, then it will be considered *istiḥãzah*.

When using skin patches which stop periods for life, spotting may still occasionally occur. If it occurs at the same time as what your monthly cycle used to be, then it will be considered as *ḥayz*, otherwise it will be considered to be *istiḥãzah*.

# 4. Categories of *Ḥã'iz*

According to the *sharī'ah*, all women are not the same as far as the rules of menstruation are concerned. By taking into consideration the difference in the regularity of time, and the number of days of monthly cycles, and their irregularity, women can be divided into three main groups:

### 1.  A Beginner *(Mubtadi'a):*
A girl who sees menstruation for the first time.

### 2.  Regular Period *(Zãtu 'l-'ãdah):*
A woman who experiences menstruation regularly at a fixed time of the month or for a fixed number of days, or both.

If a woman has two consequent periods with regularity in time of their occurrence and duration, then she is a *zãtu 'l-'ãdah* – a woman who has formed a regular pattern for her monthly periods.

On the other hand, if a woman with a regular pattern discovers that her regular pattern for menstruation has changed, and this happens for two consequent months, then she should follow the new pattern.

Women with regular patterns can be of three groups:

## Group A

Periods occur at a **fixed time,** for a **fixed duration**.

For example, starting on the 1st day of her cycle, lasting for 7 days continuously, or with a brief pause on the 4th day.

## Group B

Periods occur at a **fixed time,** no fixed duration.

For example, on the 1st day of every cycle but sometimes for 4 days and at other times for 7 days.

## Group C

Periods occur not at a fixed time, but does have a **fixed duration**.

For example, she has her periods for 4 days but not at a fixed time; sometimes on the 1st day of the monthly cycle and sometimes on the 4th day of the monthly cycle.

### 3.  Irregular Period *(Muẓṭariba):*

A woman who does not have her periods with regularity in timing **or** duration, as in a woman who has an irregular pattern for her monthly periods.

For example, a woman has her one period on the 1st day of her cycle for five days, her second period on the 5th day of her cycle for three days, and her third period on the 10th day of her cycle for four days.

*****

**In summary,** there are 3 categories of period types, with the regular category having 3 sub-sections.

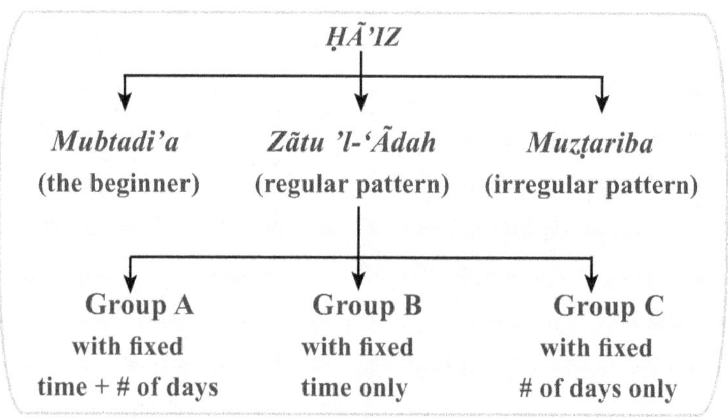


# 5. Entering Puberty

A girl who reaches the age of puberty and sees her menstruation for the first time is known as *mubtadi'a* – the beginner.

If a beginner sees blood with **all** three signs present for **more than three** and **less than ten days**, then it is menstruation.

But if a beginner sees blood for **more than ten days,** then there are a few possibilities:

**1.** The blood had **all** three signs for some days, and then **without** some or all signs for some other days, then the days with all signs is menstruation and the others are *istiḥãzah*.

**2.** The blood had all three signs during the entire flow but with a **difference in the intensity of colour.** For example, some days it had a black colour and some other days it had a red or dark red colour. In this case, the flow with black colour will be considered menstruation and the others will be considered *istiḥāzah*.

**3.** If the entire flow was **without** all three signs, or the flow with all three signs was less than three days, then the entire flow will be considered *istiḥāzah*.

**4.** If the blood had all **three signs during the entire flow,** then the beginner has to follow the number-pattern of the women in her immediate family if possible (e.g., her mother, sister, etc). For example, if her mother's monthly period occurs for six days, then she should consider the six days as menstruation and the remaining days as *istiḥāzah*.

But if the women in a beginner's family differ in the duration of their monthly periods, or she has no immediate female family members, then during the first month she should observe six or seven days as menstruation and act on precaution up to the tenth day. (Acting on precaution means refraining from those actions that are forbidden to a woman in the state of menses.) In the following months she should observe the first three days as menstruation and act on precaution up to the sixth or seventh day. This alternate pattern should be continued until she forms a regular pattern of her own.

Note that a beginner should not follow the pattern of her relative who is close to the age of menopause.

# 6. Regular Patterns - General Rules

Women with regular patterns in **Group A** (those who have periods of a fixed time and days) **and Group B** (only fixed time), must observe the rules of menstruation as soon as they see the blood.

It makes no difference whether it starts on the fixed day, or one or two days before or after it, even if all three signs of menstrual flow are not present.

Of course, if she discovers later that it was not menstruation (for example, the blood stopped on the second day), then she will have to perform her *ṣalāt* which she had not performed during the two days as *qazā*.

* * * * *

If a woman with a regular pattern in **Group C** (those who only have a fixed number of days) sees blood, then there are two situations:

1. If the blood holds **all** three signs of menstrual flow, then they should observe the rules of menstruation.

2. If the discharge does **not** have all three signs, then it will be regarded as *istiḥāza,* not menstruation.

* * * * *

## Variety of Situations for Groups A & B:

**(1)** When a woman with regular periods sees blood

*many* **days before or after** the fixed time, and it has all three signs, then it is menstruation; otherwise it will be regarded as *istiḥāza.* This is shown in the charts below. (Refer to the 'How to Read This Book' section at the beginning to understand the charts.)

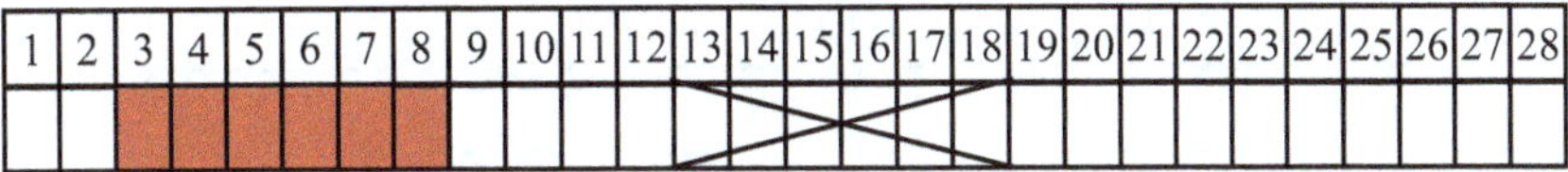

with 3 signs = *ḥayz*
without 3 signs = *istiḥāza*

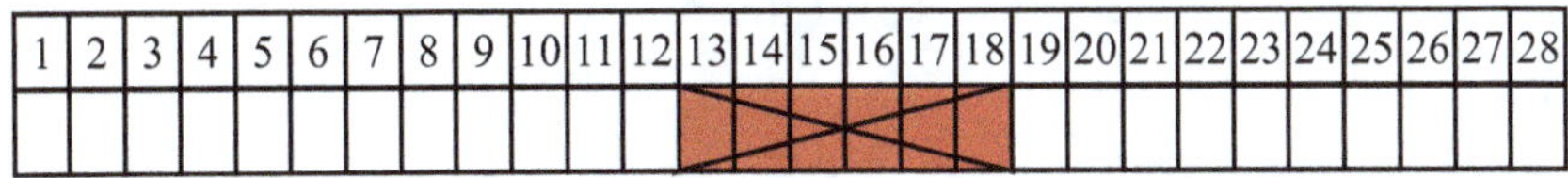

with 3 signs = *ḥayz*
without 3 signs = *istiḥāza*

* * * * *

**(2)** But as mentioned above, if a woman with regular periods sees blood **during** the fixed time, it is *ḥayz* even if it does not have the three signs.

with or without 3 signs = *ḥayz*

* * * * *

**(3)** If a woman with a regular pattern sees blood for three days, and then it stops for some days, and returns for three more days – then both flows of blood and the pause between them will be considered *ḥayz* only if the following

2 conditions are met:

i. the total days of the two flows and the pause between them is less than ten days

ii. all these days are within the fixed time and fixed number of days of the woman's menses.

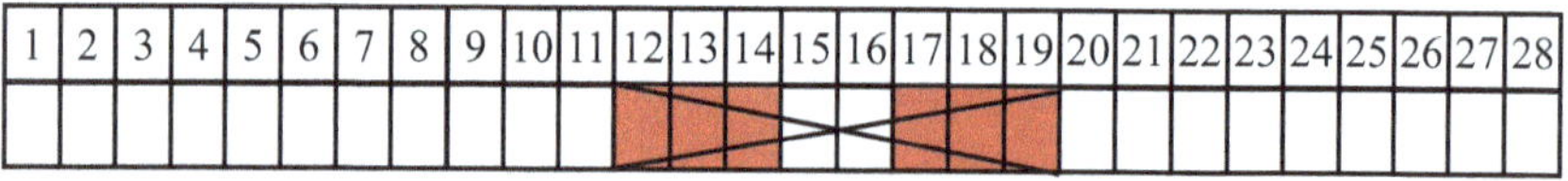

the total of 2 flows & the pause is ten days or less
+ all these days are within the fixed time
= *ḥayz*[1]

* * * * *

**(4)** In the following three cases as well, the two flows of blood and the pause between them will be counted as *ḥayz*:

i. If one of the flows started a day or two before the fixed time.

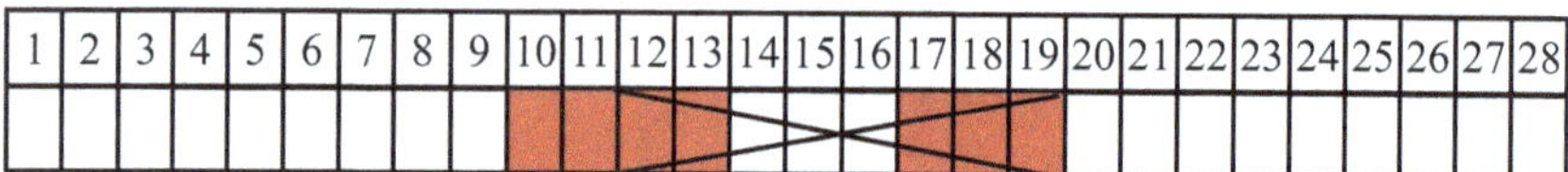

both flows and the pause = *ḥayz*

ii. If both flows started outside the fixed time but both had the three signs of menstrual flow.

with 3 signs = *ḥayz*
(if it was without 3 signs = *istiḥāza)*

---

1   Sistāni: Based on obligatory precaution, during the pause, she should fulfills the prayers and fasts.

**iii.** If one flow started outside the fixed time with all three signs while the other flow started in the fixed time, regardless of signs.

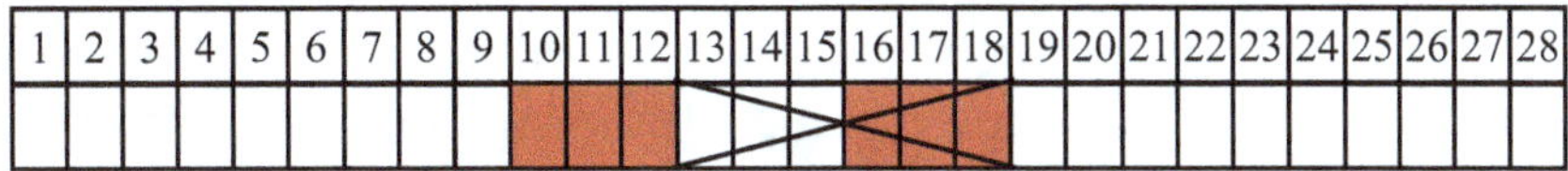

the 1st flow with 3 signs = *ḥayz*
the 1st flow without 3 signs = *istiḥãza*

But if one or both flows did not have all three signs of menstruation and none of them occurred in the fixed time, then the flow with all three signs is menstruation and the one without them is *istiḥãza*.

**(5)** If the total days of both flows is **more than ten and the pause between them is less than ten days,** then the following procedure is to be followed:

**i.** If only one of the flows was in the fixed time, that one will be considered *ḥayz* and the other one *istiḥãza*.

**ii.** In a case where none of the flows occurred in the fixed time, then

**(a)** if one had all three signs but the other did not, then the one with the signs will be *ḥayz* and the other *istiḥãza*.

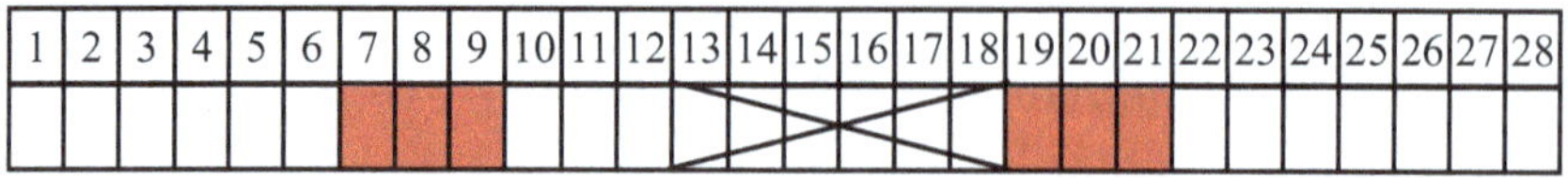

with 3 signs = *ḥayz*      without 3 signs = *istiḥāza*

**(b)** if both flows had all three signs, then the first will be considered *ḥayz* and the other will be considered *istiḥāza*.

1st with 3 signs = *ḥayz*      2nd with 3 signs = *istiḥāza*

* * * * *

**(6)** If the pause between the **two flows of blood was ten days or more,** then in the following two cases they will be considered two separate menstruations, while in the third case, it is *istiḥāza*:

**i.** if both flows had all three signs:

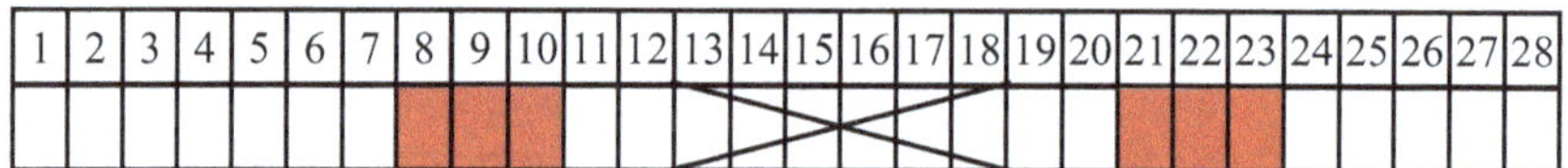

with 3 signs = two separate *ḥayz*
(if it was without 3 signs = two separate *istiḥāza)*

**ii.** if one was in the fixed time, while the other had the three signs.

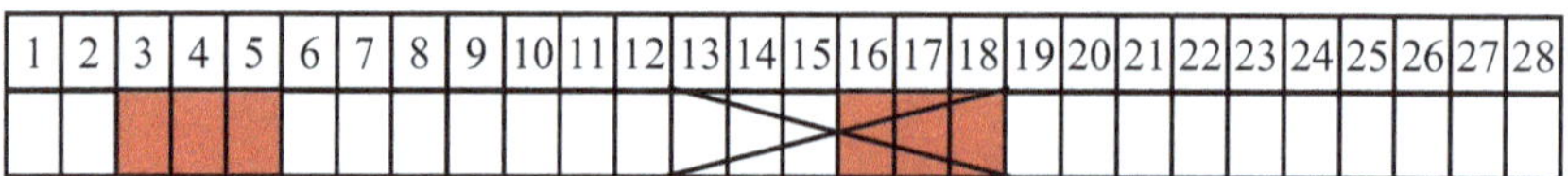

with 3 signs = *ḥayz*      with 3 signs = *ḥayz*
(without 3 signs = *istiḥāza)*    (without 3 signs = *ḥayz)*

**iii.** If both blood flows occurred outside the fixed time and both were without all three signs, then both will be counted as _istiḥāza_.

＊ ＊ ＊ ＊ ＊

## Group C:

Group C are those women whose patterns are of a fixed number of days only, even if they occur at different moments of the month.

If a **woman with a regular pattern of Group C sees blood for more than ten days,** then she should consider her fixed number of days as menstruation, even if it is without all three signs; the remaining days should be considered as _istiḥāza,_ even if it is with all three signs.

However if both flows, with and without signs, can be counted as one _ḥayz,_ then she should do so. For example, she saw her first flow according to her pattern for three days, then a pause for four days and started again with all three signs for three days, this makes a total of ten days. However if it continued without the three signs afterwards, then she would count the first flow, the intervening pause, and the second flow of three days (with the signs) as _ḥayz,_ and the remaining period as _istiḥāza._

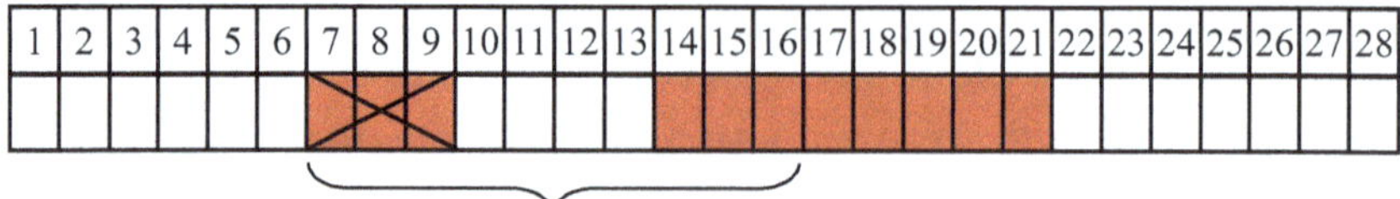

1$^{st}$ flow + pause + 3 days of 2nd flow with 3 signs = 1 *ḥayz*[1]
Later part of 2$^{nd}$ flow without 3 signs = *istiḥāza*

* * * * *

**If you aren't sure if the bleeding has stopped:**

If the blood stops before ten days and a woman is uncertain whether it has stopped completely, then she should examine herself by inserting a folded piece of toilet paper (bathroom tissue) inside her vagina and leave it there for a minute or so. While examining oneself, it is better "to stand upright leaning on a wall, etc, and lift up one leg and then insert the cotton [or toilet paper/bathroom tissue] into the vagina."[2] Then she should take it out gently.

If the toilet paper comes out dry, she should consider herself pure and perform *ghuslu 'l-ḥayz* (unless the pause during menstrual flow is normal in her case).

If the toilet paper comes out stained with blood, the rules differ slightly for the different categories of *ḥā'iz:*

**i.** A beginner, a woman with irregular periods, or a woman with regular patterns who normally has periods for 10 days: If they examine themselves and find that the toilet paper is stained, then they should consider themselves as *ḥā'iz* up to a maximum of ten days, or less if the blood stops earlier.

---

1 Sistāni: Based on obligatory precaution, during the pause, she should fulfills the prayers and fasts.

2 As explained by Imām as-Sādiq (a.s.). See al-'Āmilī, *op. cit.*, vol. 2, p. 562.

**ii.** A woman who has periods regularly for less than ten days: If she examines herself during her fixed numbers of days and finds the toilet paper stained, then she should consider herself *ḥā'iz.*

**iii.** A woman who is uncertain whether the period has stopped or not: If she examines herself outside her fixed numbers of days and finds the toilet paper stained, she should consider herself as *ḥā'iz* for up to ten days or until she finds herself pure.

If a woman who is uncertain does not examine herself and performs *ghuslu 'l-ḥayz,* then her *ghusl* is valid only if the menstrual flow does not start again.

If she is unable to examine herself, then she should consider herself *ḥā'iz* until she is sure of her purity.

# 7. Regular Patterns - Lost Track of Your Period

## Group A:

If a woman, who has a **fixed time** for the occurrence of her periods and a **fixed number of days** for its duration, forgets her fixed time, or fixed number of days, or both, then there are a few possibilities:

    **i.** She **forgot the fixed time** but remembers the fixed number of days:

       - If she has menstrual flow for three or more days, and less than ten days, then all those days will be considered *ḥayz.*

       - If the bleeding continues for more than ten, and she

knows overall that the bleeding has coincided with the fixed time, then she should act on precaution for the whole duration of the flow even if the blood does not have the three signs of menses.

- If she does not know even roughly if the bleeding has coincided with her fixed time, then she should consider the fixed number of days (which she remembers) as menstruation, and the remaining days as *istiḥāza*.

ii. She **forgot her fixed number of days** but remembers the fixed time of occurrence:

- The blood she sees at her fixed time – with or without the three signs – will be considered menstruation if it is not for more than ten days.

- If it continues past ten days, then she should consider the probable number of days from the fixed time as menstruation and the remaining days as *istiḥāza*.

- And in this case if the probable number of days is more than seven, then she should act on precaution up to the tenth day.

iii. She **forgot both** the fixed time and the fixed number of days of her monthly periods:

(a) If the blood includes all three signs and it came for not less than three and not more than ten days, then all of it will be regarded as *ḥayz*.

- If it exceeds ten days, then the days she considers as the probable days of her monthly period will be considered as *ḥāyz* and the remaining days as *istiḥāza*.

- Again, in this case if the probable duration is

more than seven days, then it is better for her to act on precaution up to the tenth day.

**(b)** If the blood includes all three signs for some days but without them for some other days – the days with signs will be considered menstruation and the days without will be _istiḥāza_.
- If both these flows are not more than ten days combined, then it is better for her to act on precaution on the days when the blood is without the three signs.

**(c)** If the blood flows for ten days or more, and she knows overall that the bleeding has coincided with her fixed time and number of days, then she should act on precaution for the entire period – even if the blood did not have all three signs.

## Group B:

A woman who has a **fixed time** for the occurrence of her periods forgets that fixed time, then:

**i.** If she has a flow for three or more days, and less than ten days, then all those days will be considered as _hayz_.

**ii.** If it occurs for more than ten days, and she knows overall that the bleeding has coincided with her fixed time, then she should act on precaution for the whole duration of the flow, even if the blood does not have all three signs of menses.

**iii.** If she does not know even roughly if the bleeding has coincided with her fixed time, then there are two possibilities:

**(a)** If the blood flow had all three signs for some days and did not have all three signs for other days, then the days with all three signs will be considered as *ḥayz* (if they are not more than ten) and the other days will be considered as *istiḥāza*.

**(b)** If the blood had all three signs during the entire flow, or for more than ten days, then six or seven days (at her discretion) should be considered as *ḥayz* and the remaining as *istiḥāza*. In this case it is better, based on *iḥtiyāṭ*, for her to act on precaution up to the tenth day.

## Group C:

If a woman who has her periods on a **fixed number of days** but not at a fixed time, forgets the duration of her menses, then she must act as follows:

i.   After she begins keeping track, if she has a flow for three or more days, and less than ten days, then all those days will be considered as *ḥayz*.

ii.  If they are more than ten days, then the number of days which she considers as the probable duration of her menses should be counted as *ḥayz* and the remaining days will be counted as *istiḥāzah*.
If the probable duration of her menses is more than seven days, then she should act on precaution from the last probable day up to the tenth day.

# 8. Irregular Patterns

If a woman with an irregular pattern sees blood with all three signs present for more than three and less than ten days, then it is considered to be menstruation.

* * * * *

But if she sees blood for **more than ten days**, then there are a few possibilities:

1.  If the blood had **all three signs** during the entire flow, then she should consider the first six or seven days as menstruation and the remaining days as *istiḥāza*.

2.  If the blood had all three signs during the entire flow but with a **difference in intensity of colour** (some days it had a black colour and some other days it had dark red colour), then the flow with black colour will be considered menstruation and the other flow will be considered *istiḥāza*. This is as long as the black coloured flow was present for more than three days and less than ten days.

3.  If the blood had **all three signs** for more than three and less than ten days, along with other days **without the signs**, then the flow with the three signs is menstruation and the ones without them are *istiḥāza*.

4.  If the entire flow was **without all three signs** or the flow with all three signs was less than three days, then the entire flow will be considered *istiḥāza*.

# 9. Various Actions During *Ḥayz*

I have already mentioned that menstruation is neither a "curse on women" nor is it related to the so-called "original sin of Eve".

Menstruation is the flow of blood; and blood, according to the *sharī'ah*, is a ritually unclean *(najis)* substance. Thus, menstruation is also considered *najis*. However, the ritual impurity of menstruation in no way prevents a woman from living a normal life at home, at work, or in the community.

A person asked Imām Ja'far aṣ-Ṣādiq (a.s.) about a woman giving water to a man while she has a monthly period. The Imām said, "One of the wives of the Prophet (s) was pouring water on him and serving him a drink while she was on her monthly period." In another tradition, Imām Muḥammad al-Bāqir (a.s.) narrates that the Prophet (s) said to one of his wives, "Serve me a drink." She said, "I am on my monthly period." The Prophet said, "Is your menstruation in your hand?!"[1]

These two narrations are sufficient to show that the ritual impurity of menstruation does not prevent a woman from living a normal life with her family and friends. Even the clothes, bedsheets, towels, etc used by a *ḥãiz* are not considered impure, unless they come into contact with *najãsat*.

* * * * *

## Forbidden Acts for the *Ḥã'iz*:

There are certain acts of worship and religous items in Islam which are so sacred that a Muslim, whether man or

---

1    Al-'Ãmilī, *op. cit.,* vol. 2, p. 595.

woman, cannot perform or handle them unless he or she is in the state of ritual purity. It is only in relation to these acts that a menstruating woman, just like a *junub* man, is forbidden from performing them. It is not a discriminating factor particularly regarding females, rather it is regarding certain forms of *najāsat* with either gender. Those forbidden acts are outlined below.

## 1. The Qur'ãn:

**(a)** It is forbidden to **touch** the writing of the Qur'ãn. Touching the Qur'ãn on a phone is permissible as one is not touching the actual writing.

Wearing a ring is permissible, however if it has inscriptions carved on the stone containing Qur'ãnic verses, one must avoid touching the wording.

**(b)** It is also forbidden to **recite** those verses of the Qur'ãn in which *sajdah* (prostration) is *wãjib*:

1.  verse 15 of chapter 32 (as-Sajdah);
2.  verse 37 of chapter 41 (Fussilat / Ḥa Mīm Sajdah);
3.  verse 62 of chapter 53 (an-Najm);
4.  verse 19 of chapter 96 (al-'Alaq).

It is better not to recite even a single verse from these four chapters.

**(c)** It is also forbidden, on the basis of precaution, **to touch** the names and attributes of Allãh even outside the Qur'ãn, in Arabic or any other language. It is better to include the names of all prophets, the Imams of Ahlul Bayt and Lady Fāṭimah in this prohibition.

Wearing a ring is permissible, however if it has

inscriptions carved on the stone containing any of the above, you must avoid touching the wordings.

## 2. The Mosque *(Masjid):*

**(a)** Entering or staying in a **mosque**.
A *ḥā'iz* is not allowed to enter or stay in a mosque.

It is necessary to clarify that a mosque, i.e., *masjid,* is different from the religious centers which are usually known as *husayniyya, imāmbārgah, matam,* etc. The prohibitions, and requirements of ritual purity, do not apply to such centres. So no female should be prevented from taking part in religious gatherings because of her menses – that is a personal matter and no one has the right to question her about her monthly cycle.

See more on this under "Recommendations" further in this chapter.

A *ḥā'iz* may pass through the mosque, only by entering from one door and leaving from another. If a person does stay in a mosque in the state of *hayz* or *janābah,* there is no *kaffāra* due, however one should seek forgiveness for ignoring the sanctity of a masjid.

However, in the following three places, one cannot even pass through the mosque:

**i.** Masjidu 'l-Ḥarām in Mecca
**ii.** Masjidu 'n-Nabī in Medina
**iii.** On the basis of precaution, the prohibition also covers shrines of the Imāms of Ahlul Bayt

As the *ḥā'iz* is not allowed to enter any mosque, naturally she cannot do circumambulation *(ṭawāf)* of the Ka'bah, nor can she observe *i'tikāf* (temporary spiritual retreat of at least three days inside a masjid).

**(b)** Placing something inside a mosque, even if the _ḥā'iz_ individual is standing outside. She may remove an item from the mosque, provided she does not enter it. This is also true for a _junub_ individual.

An important note regarding shrines: The prohibition of entering or staying in a shrine only apply to the inner section of the building which contains the _dharīh_ (tomb), and not the surrounding halls and courtyards. Therefore, a _ḥā'iz_ can enter the overall compound and perform her _ziyãrat_ from the courtyard or the surrounding halls, but she cannot go inside the inner chamber containing the _dharīh_.

## 3. Ritual Acts:

**(a)** Ritual Prayers _(Şalãt):_

A _ḥā'iz_ woman is excused from ṣalãt because she does not have an important qualification for ṣalãt, i.e., ritual purity _(ṭahãrat)_. She does **not** have to perform them later as _qazã_.

Imãm 'Ali Razã (a.s.) said, "When a woman has her monthly period, she does not...pray because she is in the state of impurity (of blood), and Allãh likes to be formally worshipped only by a person in state of purity."[1]

We can appreciate the words in the Qur'ãn where Allãh says, _"Allãh does not desire to make any impediment for you; He only desires to purify you, and that He may complete His blessings upon you; hopefully you will be thankful (to Him)"_ (The Qur'ãn 5:6).

---

1    Ibid., p. 586.

**(b)** Fasting *(Ṣawm):*

Likewise, a *ḥā'iz* is excused from fasting; however, she has to fast after the month of Ramadhān as *qazã*.

In his answer to a question asked by a man named Abū Baṣīr, Imãm Ja'far aṣ-Ṣãdiq (a.s.) said, "Fasting is just for one month in a year while *ṣalãt* is every day and night. That is why Allãh ordered that the fasts (missed by a *ḥā'iz* woman in Ramadhān) be repaid as *qazã*, while He did not order her to perform *qazã* of the *ṣalãts* (missed during *ḥayz*)."[1]

So if a woman's period starts at night time, before dawn, or anytime during the next day while fasting, then her fast of that day will not be valid; even if it is just before maghrib time. In other words, she is excused from fasting from that day till her *ḥayz* stops. And when it stops, then she must perform the *ghuslu 'l-ḥayz* before dawn of the next day and fast normally.

* * * * *

## Recommended Acts for the *Ḥã'iz*:

Being in the state *ḥayz* does not mean a *ḥā'iz* loses her spirituality. It is recommended *(mustaḥab)* for a *ḥā'iz* to change her sanitary product at the time of every prayer, perform *wuzū'*, sit on her prayer rug facing the qiblah, and recite *du'ãs* for the duration of a normal prayer. It is better for her to recite *tasbīḥãt arba'ah* (the 4 praises of God):

*subḥãn Allãhi, wal-ḥamdu lil-lãhi,*
*wa lã ilãha il lal-lãhu, wal-lãhu akbar*

---

1    Ibid., p. 591.

"Praise be to Allãh, thanks be to Allãh,
and there is no god but Allãh, and Allãh is the Great."

There is also no issue in participating in rituals such as *laylatu 'l-qadr*, *ziyãrat 'Ãshurã'*, *"amman yujiboo" du'ã*, etc. However, performing the recommended *ṣalãt* associated with these acts, or reciting a Qur'ãnic verse where *sajdah* is *wãjib*, are not valid.

Note that she can also participate in funeral prayers.

## Discouraged Acts for the *Ḥã'iz*:

It is discouraged *(makrūh)* for a *ḥã'iz* woman to recite more than 7 Qur'ãnic verses, as well as to keep, carry or touch the border of the pages of the Qur'ãn, or the blank space between the lines.

It is *makrūh* for her to colour her hair during menstruation.

There is no issue with having a *nikãḥ* performed during a cycle, though consummation must wait until she is ritually pure.

A divorce is not valid if done during the period, or post-partum bleeding.

## Cultural Taboos in Society:

This list of forbidden and discouraged acts during menstruation should dispel the superstitions that some communities have regarding depriving a *ḥã'iz* from taking part in preparing and eating the food of religious gatherings (known as *nazr* in the South Asian culture). If it is recommended for a *ḥã'iz* to sit on her *muṣalla* (prayer rug) at the time of *ṣalāt* and recite *tasbīḥ* and *du'ã,* then why can she not partake in preparing, cooking and eating food in religious gatherings? The monthly cycle is a personal matter and asking another woman "are you *ṭāhir / pãk?*" is inappropriate. Remember the *ḥadīth* quoted earlier when the Prophet asked one of his wives for a drink, and she replied, "I am in my menses." The Prophet said, "Is your period in your hand?" as a way to indicate that her state of purity does not matter for this context.

* * * * *

At the end of this chapter I would like to present the following verses from the Bible, to demonstrate the stark difference in accomodations, so that the reader may appreciate the laws of Islam. The Bible, in the Book of Leviticus, says:

> When a woman has a discharge, her discharge being blood from her body, she shall remain in her impurity for seven days; whoever touches her shall be unclean until evening. Anything that she lies on during her impurity shall be unclean; and anything that she sits on shall be unclean. Anyone who touches her bedding shall wash his clothes, bathe in water, and remain unclean until evening; and anyone who touches any object on which she has sat shall wash his clothes, bathe in water, and remain unclean until evening. Be it the bedding or be it the object on which she has sat, on touching it he shall be unclean until evening. And if a man lies with her, her impurity is communicated to him; he shall be unclean seven days, and any bedding on which he lies shall become unclean.

When she becomes clean of her discharge, she shall count off seven days, and after that she shall be clean. On the eighth day she shall take two turtledoves or two pigeons, and bring them to the priest at the entrance of the Tent of Meeting. The priest shall offer the one as a sin offering and the other as a burnt offering; and the priest shall make expiation on her behalf, for her unclean discharge, before the Lord."
(Lev. 15:19-30)

We can appreciate the words in the Qur'ān where Allāh says, *"Allāh does not desire to make any impediment for you; He only desires to purify you, and that He may complete His blessings upon you; hopefully you will be thankful (to Him)"* (The Qur'ān 5:6).

Taking heed of what the Qur'ān, the *sunnah* of the Prophet (s) and the Imams of Ahlul Bayt (a) have said, these teachings will aid a menstruating woman to live her life normally in society, without being put through undue hardship or embarrasment.

# 10. Sex & Menstruation

By considering the discomfort of women during monthly periods, Islam has forbidden both the husband and wife from sexual intercourse during the menstruation.

The Qur'ān says, *"They ask you about menstruation. (O Muḥammad) tell (them that) menstruation is a discomfort (for the women, it is a period when they pass through physical and emotional tension. Therefore,) do not establish sexual relations with them during the menses, and (again you are reminded that) do not approach them (sexually) until the blood stops. Then when they have cleansed themselves, you (are permitted to) go into them as Allāh has commanded you (through nature)." (2:222)*

However, it is permissible for a husband and wife to enjoy each other physically during menses, other than the act of intercourse itself. A husband may play with other parts of his wife's body other than the vagina and anus during a period. Again, it is better not to play with her body between the navel and knees. See my book *Marriage & Morals in Islam.*

If a man who is engaged in sexual intercourse with his wife discovers that her period has started, he should immediately withdraw himself from her.

Based on the above verse (*"until the blood stops"*), once the blood has stopped, intercourse becomes lawful even if the wife has not performed her *ghusl.* However on the basis of the subsequent sentence (*"then when they have cleansed themselves"*), most jurists say that it is better to refrain from intercourse until she performs *ghusl* or at least washes her private parts.

'Alī bin Yaqṭīn asked Imām al-Kāzim (a.s.) about a man having intercourse with his wife when her period has stopped but she has not yet performed *ghusl.* The Imām said, "There is no harm in it; but (intercourse) after the *ghusl* is preferable to me."[1]

If bleeding continues for longer than 10 days, then it is considered *istiḥāza,* during which time intercourse is permissible. (i.e. after ten days.)

---

1    Ibid., p. 573.

If spotting occurs and a woman is unsure whether it was *istiḥāza* or *hayz*, and engages in intercourse, and later confirms it was *hayz*, then both *ghuslu 'l-janābah* and *ghuslu 'l-hayz* must be delayed until the end of *hayz*. *Ghuslu 'l-janābah* will be sufficient for both. Because of the doubt between *istiḥāza* or *hayz*, there is no *kaffāra* required.

If a woman is in the state of *janābah* but has not yet performed *ghusl* and her menstruation begins, she must wait until the end of *hayz*. *Ghuslu 'l-janābah* will be sufficient for both *ghusls*.

Though it is forbidden for both the husband and wife to indulge in intercourse during *hayz* (before 10 days), **kaffāra** is recommended, not mandatory. If it occured during the early days of the cycle, then *kaffāra* is equal to 3.5 grams of a gold coin; during the middle of the cycle, it is 1.75 grams, and towards the end of the cycle, it is 0.875 grams.

# 11. *Ṣalāt* & Menstruation

**Pre-*Ṣalāt*:**

If the time for a particular *ṣalāt* has already begun and a woman fears that by delaying the *ṣalāt* her period may start, then it is *wājib* on her to perform that *ṣalāt* immediately.

If the time for a particular *ṣalāt* has already begun and the woman did not pray until her period started, then she has to perform that *ṣalāt* as *qazā* any time after the menstruation stops and *ghusl-e hayz* has been performed.

**Mid-*Ṣalāt*:**

If a woman sees or feels for certain that bleeding has started while she is performing *ṣalāt*, she should stop her *ṣalāt* immediately as she is now in the state of *ḥayz*. If she discovers later on that it was not *ḥayz* (e.g., the blood stopped on the second day), then she should perform *qazā* of the *ṣalāt* which she has missed.

If a woman who is engaged in *ṣalāt* doubts whether or not her period has started, her doubt will have no effect on the *ṣalāt*. She may continue praying. However, if she discovers later on that her period had actually begun, then her *ṣalāt* will have become invalid, and there will be no *qazā* required.

**_Ṣalāt_ Time Ending Soon:**

If a woman's menses has ended and she has enough time to perform *ghuslu 'l-ḥayz* and pray at least one *rak‘at* in time – then it is *wājib* on her to do so. If she does not perform the *ghusl* and then pray, then it is *wājib* on her to perform its *qazā* later on.

For example, the time of *‘aṣr* prayer is ending at 5 p.m. and a woman's period stops at 4 p.m. In this case, she has enough time to perform *ghuslu 'l-ḥayz* and pray *‘aṣr ṣalāt*. If she does not do so, then it will be *wājib* for her to perform *ṣalāt* of *‘aṣr* as *qazā*.

If a woman's menses has ended while she does not have enough time to perform *ghusl* and pray at least one *rak‘at* in time – then it is obligatory, on the basis of precaution, for her to perform *tayammum* instead of *ghusl*, and pray.[1] If she

---

1    Khumayni: it is not *wājib*.

does not do so, then it is *wājib*, on the basis of precaution for her to perform that *ṣalāt* as *qazā*.[1]

Likewise, if a woman's menses has ended and she has enough time to perform *ghusl* and pray at least one *rak'at* in time, however she is unable to do so in certain situations, then she should perform *tayammum* and pray accordingly.

For example, a woman's period ends while she is at her workplace at 3 p.m. and the time of *Zuhr/'Aṣr* prayers end at 5:10 p.m., however she does not get off of work until 5 p.m. She can perform *tayammum* instead and then pray.

# 12. *Ghuslu 'l-Ḥayz*

When a woman's menses has ended, it is *wājib* upon her to perform *ghusl,* the major ritual ablution. A regular shower does not substitute the ritual *ghusl*. Apart from sexual intercourse, all the acts forbidden to a women will remain so until she performs *ghuslu 'l-ḥayz*.

If she is are required to perform *ghuslu 'l-janābah*, then that one *niyyat* and *ghusl* will also suffice for *ghuslu 'l-ḥayz*.

She should ensure to keep the correct *ghusl* in mind during her *niyyat*. Either *ghuslu 'l-ḥayz, ghuslu 'l-istiḥāza,* or *ghuslu 'l-janābat*.

If, due to circumstances and not negligence, one does not have enough time to perform *ghusl* before *ṣalāt* time ends, one may perform *tayammum* to pray, and then perform *ghusl* as soon as possible.

---

1    Khū'ī: It is not *wājib* to do the *qazā*.

As mentioned earlier, *tahārat* and *ghusl* are not required for doing *ṣalāt* of a funeral (*Ṣalātul Mayyit*).

The manner of performing *ghuslu 'l-ḥayz* is the same as the method explained in my book *Ritual & Spiritual Purity*. For the convenience of the reader, I will also explain the manner of performing *ghusl* here.

Nail polish, fake nails, fake lashes, etc must be removed before *ghusl*. Nail polish is a barrier for water in *ghusl*, therefore even if it is on one toe, the *ghusl* is invalid and it has to be redone after removing the nail polish. Note that according to Āyatullāh Sistāni, while wiping the foot in *wuzū'*, doing it simply from any one toe to the ankle is sufficient. This has prompted some to put nail polish on all their toes except one, usually the baby toe – so they can easily do *wuzū'* with nail polish on. However this only applies to *wuzū'*; for *ghusl*, nail polish on any finger or toe is a barrier and would make the *ghusl* invalid. Moreover, 'breathable' nail polish is not acceptable as it is still a barrier for water.

Jewelry that will be a barrier must be removed. Jewelry that won't prevent water contact is permissible, such as a necklace chain that can be lifted or shifted.

It is not necessary to remove pubic hair after *ḥayz*, or before *ghusl*.

In doing *ghusl*, the hair that is close to the scalp must be washed. However, it is not necessary to wash the entire strand of long hair. So if water reaches the skin of the scalp in a way that the entire hair does not become wet, the *ghusl* is still valid. Tying your hair in a bun or an updo is also permissible as long as water reaches the scalp underneath the hairstyle.

There are two methods of performing the major ritual ablution: *Ghusl Tartībī* and *Ghusl Irtimāsi*.

**1. *Ghusl Tartībi*:** This is the common and preferred method.

First, cleanse one's body to remove any *najāsat*, and perform your *niyyat*.

The body has to be washed in three stages, under running water (e.g. under the shower):

1. Wash the head and the neck
2. Wash the right side of the body, from the shoulders to the foot
3. Wash the left side of the body

**Note for followers of Āyatullāh Sistāni:** While doing *ghusl tartībi*, once you have washed your head and neck, you should either turn the tap off momentarily, or move away from under the running water and then return to wash the rest of the body (as opposed to washing the right and left sides separately). This is based on *iḥtiyāṭ wājib*; and in such a situation he gives you the option of referring to the ruling of the second-best mujtahid in this particular case. So you can refer to Āyatullāh Waḥīd Khurāsāni or other living *marāji'* who say you perform ghusl without stepping away or turning the tap off.

**2. *Ghusl Irtimāsi*:**

In this type of *ghusl*, after all *najāsat* has been removed, and making the *niyyat*, the whole body should be completely immersed in water at once, not gradually. Such a type of *ghusl* can only be done in a large body of water such as a swimming pool, a river, lake, etc, but not a bathtub. One has to make sure that all the parts of her body, including the skin under the hair, have been washed.

Note that *ghusl tartībī* is preferred to *ghusl irtimãsi.*

If any *najãsat* or nail polish is noticed after performing the *ghusl*, it must be cleaned off and the *ghusl* must be repeated again.

* * * * *

There is no need to wash any clothes, bedsheets, towels etc used during the menses, unless they came in contact with blood. The sweat or saliva of a menstruating girl or woman is not considered *najis.*

* * * * *

### *Wuzū'* after *Ghusl 'l-ḥayz*:

For the followers of Āyatullāhs Khū'ī and Sistāni: all *wãjib ghusls* exempt the doer from having to perform *wuzū'*. However, in the case of *ghuslu 'l-ḥayz*, it is *recommended* to do *wuzū'* before doing the *ghusl*.

For the followers of Āyatullāh Khumayni: it is a *must* to do *wuzū'* before or after *ghuslu 'l-ḥayz*.

* * * * *

According to Āyatullāh Khū'ī and Sistāni, all the confirmed recommended (*sunnat*) *ghusls* also suffice the doer from *wuzū'* such as:

- *Ghuslu 'l-Jum'a.* It can be done:
  - from dawn to dusk on Friday
  - As *qazã* till the sunset of Saturday
  - On Thursday if a person feels that they will not be able to do it on Friday
- *Ghusls* for the following eves of Ramadhãn:
  - 1st, 17th, 19th, 21st, 23rd and 24th
- *Ghusl* for 'īdul fiṭr (fajr to dusk)
- *Ghusl* for 'idul adha (fajr to dusk)
- *Ḥajj Ghusls* for:
  - *Tawriya* & 'Arafah day (8th & 9th Dhul Hijja)
  - *Ihram*
  - Entering the holy perimeter of Mecca
  - Entering the city of Mecca
  - *Ziyãrat* of, or entering inside, the Ka'bah
  - *Qurbani* in *ḥajj*
  - *Halq* (shaving in *ḥajj*)
- *Ghusls* related to the *ziyãrat* of the Prophet
  - Entering the city of Medina
  - Entering Masjidu 'n-Nabi
  - Farewell *Ziyãrat* of his shrine

Note that according to Āyatullāh Khumayni, these *sunnat ghusls* do not suffice the doer from *wuzū'*.

# Part Two

# *Istiḥāza*:
# Irregular Bleeding

## 1. Definition of *Istiḥāza*

You have come across the word *istiḥāza* many times in the first part of this book. In this section we shall exclusively discuss the concept of *istiḥāza*.

**The Definition:** *Istiḥāza* is usually translated as "irregular menstruation." But this translation is incorrect, because it may create confusion with *muztariba*: "a woman whose menstrual pattern is irregular;" and also because *istiḥāza* is not considered menstruation at all.

In Islamic terminology, *istiḥāza* means *any* blood discharged from a woman that is **not** from menstruation, loss of virginity, post-natal bleeding or internal injury. A woman who is in the state of *istiḥāza* is known as *mustaḥāza*.

**The 4 Signs of *Istiḥāza*:**
    (a) cool temperature
    (b) yellow in colour
    (c) thin in substance
    (d) discharged without pressure or burning sensation

These 4 signs are the opposite of the signs of menstruation.

Although these are the signs which usually appear in *istiḥāza,* sometimes it is quite possible for it to appear without some, or even all of them.

Unlike *ḥayz,* there is **no minimum or maximum duration** for the discharge of *istiḥāza.* Neither is there any specific age in a woman's life-time during which it appears – it can occur before a girl turns nine years old, or after a woman has entered the age of menopause.[1] Nor is there a minimum duration necessary between two occurrences of *istiḥāza.*

## 2. Three Types of *Istiḥāza*

By considering the amount of blood in *istiḥāza,* it is divided into three categories: *qalīlah, mutawassiṭah* and *kathīrah.*

**1. Slight Bleeding *(Qalīlah):*** Discharge which stains cotton, but does not penetrate it. In today's context, this means spotting discharge which causes a pad to be changed only once a day.

---

1    According to Āyatullāh Khumayni and Waḥīd Khurāsāni the discharge of blood before the age of nine and after menopause is not considered *isthihāza.* In other words, the rulings of *ishtihāza* would not apply in these cases.

     Āyatullāh Sistāni agrees with this view but says that on the basis of precaution, a woman who sees blood after the age of sixty should do prayers and fasting as per the rules of *istihāzah* regarding *wuzū'* and *ghusl.*

**2. Medium Bleeding *(Mutawassiṭah)*:** Discharge which penetrates cotton but does not flow out from it. In today's context, this means discharge which causes a pad to be changed every 4-5 hours.

**3. Profuse Bleeding *(Kathīrah)*:** Discharge which penetrates cotton and flows out from it. In today's context, this means discharge which causes a pad to be changed every 2 hours or less.

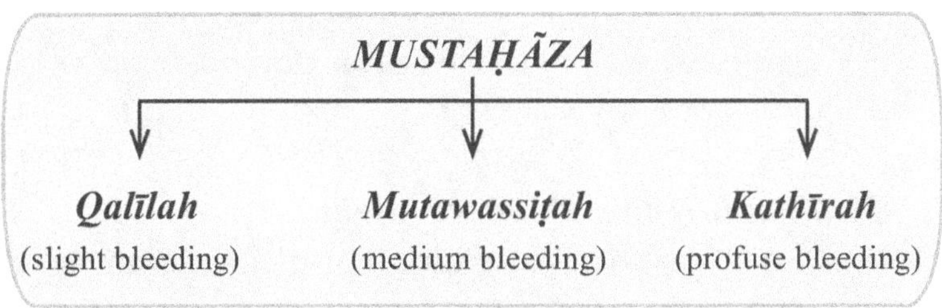


It is quite normal for *istiḥāza* discharge to change from one level to another; for example, in the beginning it could be slight, and then it becomes profuse, or vice versa.

A *mustaḥāza* woman must examine herself to determine whether her discharge is of a slight, medium or profuse level, so that she can follow the rules accordingly.

# 3. *Ṣalāt* of a *Mustaḥāza*

Istiḥāza is a ritual impurity *(najāsat)* which is different from *ḥayz*. A woman in *istiḥāza* is not exempt from *ṣalāt*. She has to pray, but the validity of her prayers depends on fulfilling the additional acts which are required of her.

In this section we shall explain the rules which a *mustaḥāza* has to observe daily for her *ṣalāt*.

### Slight Bleeding (Qalīlah):

A woman with irregular bleeding of a slight level should change her sanitary pad and do **wuzū' for ṣalāt** whether it is *wājib* or *mustaḥab*.

Changing the pad and doing *wuzū'* once suffices for all prayers until the *wuzū'* becomes invalid. Therefore, it is not necessary to redo *wuzū'* or change the sanitary pad for every *ṣalāt*, though it is better to do so.[1]

> - **Change the pad & do *wuzū'* for the *ṣalāt*.**
> - **That is sufficient for subsequent prayers until the *wuzū'* becomes invalid.**

### Medium Bleeding (Mutawassiṭah):

A woman with irregular bleeding of a medium level has to perform **ghusl before the dawn prayer,** and then **for each ṣalāt** she must change her sanitary pad, and do *wuzū'*.

> - **Do one *ghusl* before dawn prayer;**
> - **Change the pad & do *wuzū'* for each of the 5 *ṣalāts*.**

If medium bleeding of *istiḥāza* starts **after the *Fajr* prayer**, then on that day it is *wājib* on the *mustaḥāza* to perform a *ghusl* before *Zuhr* prayer.

If medium bleeding of *istiḥāza* starts **after the midday prayers *(zuhr & 'aṣr)***, then it is *wājib* on her to do the *ghusl* before the *Maghrib* prayers.

If medium bleeding of *istiḥāza* starts **between *zuhr* and *'aṣr* prayers** or **between *maghrib* and *'ishā'* prayers**,

---

1    Khū'ī: In the case of slight bleeding, it is necessary to redo the *wuzū'* and change the sanitary pad for each of the 5 *ṣalāts*.

then it is *wājib* on her to perform the ghusl before *'aṣr* or *'ishā'* prayer.

If a woman sees *istiḥāza* at a medium level before the dawn prayer and does not perform *ghusl*, then she must do *ghusl* before *zuhr* prayer and repeat her dawn prayer after the *ghusl* as *qazā*.

### *Profuse Bleeding (Kathīrah):*

A woman with irregular bleeding of a profuse level must **change her sanitary pad before each of the 5 *ṣalāts* and perform three *ghusls*** – the first *ghusl* before *Fajr* prayer, the second *ghusl* before *Zuhr* and *'Aṣr* prayers, and the third *ghusl* before *Maghrib* and *'Ishā'* prayers.

It is **not *wājib*** for a woman who has profuse bleeding to perform *wuzū'* for every *ṣalāt* as the *ghusl istiḥāza kathīrah* by itself is sufficient for *ṣalāt*.

> - **Change the pad for each of the 5 *ṣalāts***
> - **and do 3 *ghusls*:**   before *Fajr*
>                            before *Zuhr*
>                            before *Maghrib*

If a woman sees irregular bleeding of a profuse level **after *Fajr* prayer**, then on that day she has to do two *ghusls* – one before *Zuhr* prayer and the other before *Maghrib* prayer.

If she sees irregular bleeding of a profuse level **after *Zuhr*/*'Aṣr* prayers**, then on that day she will have to do one *ghusl* before the *Maghrib* prayer.

If she sees irregular bleeding of a profuse level **between** *Zuhr* and *'Aṣr* prayers or **between** *Maghrib* and *'Ishā'* prayers, then on that day she has to perform *ghusl* before *'Aṣr* or *'Ishā'* prayer respectively.

A woman who has irregular bleeding of a profuse level **must combine** the *Zuhr* and *'Aṣr* prayers after the second *ghusl*, and also combine *Maghrib* and *'Ishā'* prayers after the third *ghusl*.

This means that if a woman performs *ghusl* before *Zuhr* prayer and does not recite *'Aṣr* prayers immediately afterwards, then she will have to do a separate *ghusl* for *'Aṣr* prayer also. The same rule applies if she recites the *Maghrib* and *'Ishā'* prayers separately.

If a woman finds the requirement of doing three *ghusls* in one day as extremely difficult due to ill health or feeling that it is unbearable, she will have to see if she can do the required *ghusl* or not within time of the prayer.

If she does not have the strength to do *ghusl* until the end of the prayer's time, then she should do *tayammum* instead of *ghusl*, then do *wuzū'* normally, and then do the prayer.

# 4. Fasts of a *Mustaḥāza*

A *mustaḥāza* woman has to fast like every other person. The validity of her fast at all three levels of *istiḥāza* does not depend on her performing the required *wuzū'* and *ghusls*. In other words, a *mustaḥāza*'s fasts are valid even if she does not do the *ghusl istiḥāza*.[1]

---

1    Khū'ī: The validity of fast in the case of slight bleeding depends on doing the required *wuzū'*; in the case of medium bleeding, its validity depends (on the basis of recommended precaution) on doing the required *wuzū'*'s and *ghusl*; in the case of profuse bleeding, its validity depends on doing the required *wuzū'*'s and *ghusls*.

# 5. General Rules of *Istiḥāza*

It is *wãjib* on the *mustaḥãza* to perform the prayer immediately after the *wuzū'* or *ghusl*. She is permitted to perform the recommended *(mustaḥab)* acts before or during the prayer.

If the *istiḥãza* has stopped completely and she has already performed what was required of her, then it is not *wãjib* for her to perform her prayers immediately after *wuzū'* or *ghusl*.

* * * * *

Between *ghusl* and completion of the prayers, it is *wãjib* on the *mustaḥãza* to take necessary precautions by using a sanitary pad to absorb any flow.

If she does not take necessary precautions in this matter and blood comes out during prayer, then she must repeat her prayer. In this case of negligence, if she has medium or profuse bleeding, then it is recommended (on the basis of precaution) that she repeat the *ghusl* or *ghusls*.

* * * * *

If the *istiḥãza* stops completely before she has performed the *wuzū'* or *ghusl* that was required of her, then it is *wãjib* for her to perform the acts which were required of her before her *istiḥãza* had ended.

If the blood stops during *wuzū'*, *ghusl* or *ṣalãt*, it is *wãjib* on her to perform that action again. Even if the blood stops after she has performed her prayers but there still is enough time to do *wuzū'* or *ghusl* and pray, then it is *wājib* for her to perform those acts again.

If a *mustaḥāza* knows that the bleeding will stop at a time when she will have enough time to perform her *wuzū'* or *ghusl* and pray (without making them *qazā*), then it is *wājib* for her to delay her prayers until her bleeding has ended. For example, *Zuhr* and *'Aṣr* prayers timing ends at 5:00 p.m. and she has a feeling that her bleeding will end before 3:00 p.m. In this case she should delay her *Zuhr* and *'Aṣr* prayers, and perform the *wuzū'* or *ghusl* and pray after her bleeding has ended.

If her *istiḥāza* started after the time of prayers has started and she had not yet prayed, then she will have to pray that *ṣalāt* after performing the *wuzū'* or *ghusl* which is required of her. For example, the time of *Zuhr* prayer commenced at 12:30 p.m. and her *istiḥāza* started at 3:00 p.m. In this case she had had enough time from the commencement of *Zuhr* time to perform her prayers normally. If she did not do so, then she will have to follow the rules of *istiḥāza* to perform that prayer.

## 6. Changes in levels of *Istiḥāza*

If it changes from **a lower level to a higher level** (e.g., from slight to medium bleeding, or from medium to profuse bleeding), then there are two possibilities:

**(a)** The change occurred **before** performing the acts required of her: She should perform those acts according to the rules of the higher level *istiḥāza*, and there is no need to repeat the prayer recited earlier.

**(b)** The change occurred **while** she was performing the acts which were required of her: She has to start those actions again according to the rules of the higher level *istiḥāza*. This law applies even if the change occurs during prayers.

If it changes from **a higher level to a lower level** (e.g., from profuse to medium bleeding, or from medium to slight bleeding), then the *mustaḥāza* will have to follow the rules of the higher level *istiḥāza* for the first joint set of prayers and then follow the rules of the lower level *istiḥāza* for the subsequent prayers.

For example, a *mustaḥāza kathīra* (profuse) becomes *mustaḥāza qalīlah* (medium) before *Zuhr*, then she will have to perform a *ghusl* and then pray *Zuhr* and *'Aṣr* prayer (according to the rules of *kathīrah*) but for *Maghrib* and *'Ishā'* prayers she just has to perform separate *wuzū*'s (according to the rules of *qalīlah*).

# 7. Forbidden Actions During *Istiḥāza*

Among the acts forbidden to the *ḥā'iz* and *junub*, only one is forbidden for *mustaḥāza*: She is not permitted to touch the writings of the Qur'ān before doing the required *wuzū'* and/or *ghusl*.

There is no harm if a *mustaḥāza* woman enters and stays inside a mosque or reads those parts of the Qur'ān which contain *wājib sajdahs*, or any other action. There is no restriction, whatsoever, on sexual intercourse for a *mustaḥāza* of all levels.[1]

---

1   Khū'ī: There is no restriction on sexual intercourse for a *mustaḥāza* with slight bleeding. However, in the case of medium and profuse

* * * * *

---

bleeding (based on recommended precaution) sexual intercourse is lawful only if she has done the *ghusl* or *ghusls* which are required of her.

# <u>Part Three</u>

# *Nifās*
# Childbirth Bleeding

## 1. Definition of *Nifās*

*Nifās* literally means "childbed, childbirth, parturition, lochia." In Islamic legal terminology, it means "the blood which is discharged from a woman's womb **during or after** childbirth." The time of "childbirth" refers to the time of the actual delivery of the child.

A woman in the state of *nifās* is known as *nafsā'*.

The blood discharged during labour (before the actual moments of childbirth) is **not** regarded as *nifās*.

Similarly, if a woman's water (amniotic sac) breaks, followed by some time before the actual childbirth, then that time period is **not** considered to be *nifās*.

**Duration:**
There is **no minimum duration** for *nifās*. Even if only a drop of blood is discharged during or after childbirth, it will be regarded as *nifās*.

As far as the period of occurrence is concerned, any blood which is discharged up to ten days after childbirth, or from the commencement of the bleeding, is *nifās*. So, if a woman who saw no blood during or after the childbirth sees blood nine days later, then that blood will still be regarded as *nifās*.

The **maximum duration** of *nifās* is **ten days** from the time of completion of childbirth or from the commencement of the bleeding. So, if a woman sees blood at childbirth and it continues for ten days, all those days will be *nifās*.

On the other hand, if a woman sees blood on the seventh day after the childbirth, or from the commencement of the bleeding, and then it continues for five days more, she will consider herself in *nifās* up to the end of the tenth day from the childbirth, or from the commencement of the bleeding. For the remaining period (i.e., 10th to 12th day from the childbirth) she will act on precaution – avoiding all things forbidden in *nifās* and doing all that is required in *istiḥāza*.

There is **no minimum duration required between two nifās**. For example, a woman who gave birth to twins who were born five days apart due to various circumstances, sees blood for 5 days after the first child. Then it stops, and she sees blood again after the second child's birth – the two bleedings will be counted as two separate *nifās*.

### Miscarriage:
Note that blood discharged from a woman's womb after a miscarriage is also considered *nifās* for a maximum of ten days. If bleeding continues beyond ten days, it will be considered *istiḥāza*.

If bleeding occurs leading up to a miscarriage, and it does not coincide with the woman's cycle, it will be considered *istiḥāza*. If it does coincide with the cycle, then it will be considered *ḥayz*.

An ectopic pregnancy is considered to be a miscarriage. If the fetus is removed surgically, then there is no issue of *nifās* occuring. The woman should perform *wuzū'* normally, and if any *ghusl* is required, then she should perform *tayammum*.

# 2. Three Types of *Nafsā'* Women

*Nafsā':* a woman who is going through *nifās* can be of three types:

**1.** A woman whose bleeding **does not exceed ten days**. In such a case, all the days of bleeding will be considered *nifās*.

**2.** A woman whose bleeding **exceeds ten days** and, as far as her menstrual cycles are concerned, she has **regular patterns** with a fixed number of days.

In this case the days equal to the duration of her menstruation will be regarded as *nifās* and the remaining days as *istiḥāza*.

**3.** A woman whose bleeding **exceeds ten days and she has no regular pattern.**

In this case, the first ten days will be considered as *nifās* and the remaining days will be as *istiḥāza*.

# 3. General Rules of *Nifās*

If a woman's water (amniotic sac) breaks, followed by some time before the actual childbirth, then that time period is **not** considered to be *nifās*. *Ṣalāt* during this time, be it hours or days, is obligatory. She should, to the best of her abilities and pain level, clean herself and perform *wuzū'* or *tayammum*, and then pray while seated. Refer to my book *Praying with Physical Challenges* for further information on praying methods. If this isn't possible, then she may perform *qazā* later on.

* * * * *

Any blood seen during labour (before the birth of the child) has three possibilities:

1. If it occurs during the monthly cycle time *and* has the three signs, then it is *ḥayz*;

2. If it either occurs during the monthly cycle time without signs *or* outside the cycle with the three signs, then it is *ḥayz*;

3. Outside of the above two scenarios, it will be considered as *istiḥāza*.

* * * * *

When the *nifās* stops but the *nafsā'* is **uncertain** whether or not it has stopped completely, then she should examine herself just as a *ḥā'iz* was required to do in similar circumstances. Refer to previous chapters to learn more.

* * * * *

If due to **not knowing the rules, or due to ignorance**, the woman has left her fasts and prayers after her period of *nifās* was completed as she was bleeding after ten days also, then she should make up for her fasts and prayers of those days to an extent that she becomes satisfied that she has fulfilled her obligation.

* * * * *

Suppose a *nafsā'* woman sees blood on the first day of childbirth and **then it stops and starts again** on, or before, the tenth day. In this case there are two possibilities:

**(a)** The second bleeding **does not go past the tenth day** from the commencement of the first flow—both flows and the pause between them will be regarded as one *nifās*. However, during the pause (based on precaution), she must perform her prayers and refrain from the prohibitions of *nifās*.

**(b)** The second bleeding **goes past the tenth day** from the commencement of the first flow. This has four possibilities:

    **i.** She has a **fixed number of days** for her menstrual cycles, and the second flow took place within the fixed number. For example, her menses usually continues for seven days; now she saw blood of *nifās* for two days from childbirth, then it stopped, and re-started again on the sixth day and continued, exceeding the tenth day. In this case, the first flow, the pause, and the second bleeding within the fixed number of days (i.e, up to the seventh day after childbirth), will be regarded as one *nifās* and the remaining days will be *istiḥāza*.

ii. The woman has a **fixed duration** for her menstrual cycles, **but the second flow** did not take place during the fixed duration – then the first flow will be *nifãs*, the pause will be regarded as a period of purity and the second flow will be regarded as *istiḥãza*.

iii. She does **not have a fixed pattern** for her menstrual cycles, and the second flow started **during** the fixed duration of her relatives' monthly periods – then the days equal to the duration of her relatives' monthly periods will be *nifãs* and the remaining *istiḥãza*.

If the duration of her relatives' periods is less than ten days then she should act on precaution after the last day up to the tenth day by performing the *wãjibat* and refraining from the prohibitions.

iv. She does **not have a fixed pattern** for her menstrual cycles, and the second flow started **after** the fixed duration of her relatives' monthly periods – then the first flow will be considered *nifãs;* and during the pause and second flow she should act on precaution up to the tenth day by performing the *wãjibat* and refraining from the prohibitions.

* * * * *

When **breastfeeding**, periods do not occur, but sometimes **spotting** occurs. If it occurs during the regular cycle pattern, then it is to be considered as *ḥayz* provided it is for three days or more. Otherwise, it is considered as *istiḥãza*.

* * * * *

**Question:** It said that a lady is **exempted from prayers for 40 days** after the childbirth. Is that true?

**Answer:** No, this is not true. A lady is exempted from

prayers only for 10 days after the childbirth. If the bleeding continues after 10 days, then it is considered as *istihāza* and she has to do the prayers by following the rules of *istihāza*.

**Question:** "Why are women exempt from *salāt* after childbirth for *only* 10 days when it is recognized as normal to bleed heavily for up to 6 weeks after childbirth? It feels very burdensome trying to care for a newborn and having to do *ghusl* before each *salāt*."

**Answer:** Medically speaking, bleeding is heaviest the first few days after a baby is born. After about 10 days, a woman sees less blood; she may have light bleeding or spotting for up to 6 weeks after delivery. If heavy bleeding continues after then days, then she should see her doctor.

Islam has considered the first 10 days after childbirth as *nifās* when the woman is exempted from daily prayers. For a woman who see slight bleeding after that, she will consider it as slight *istihāza* (*qalīlah*) in which she has to do wuzū' for each *salāt*.

If the post-*nifās* bleeding is heavy and coincides with the pattern of her monthly cycle, it will be considered to be her regular cycle in which she is exempted from *salāt*.

If the heavy bleeding past ten days is not within the pattern of her cycle, then it will be considered as profuse bleeding (*kathīrah*) in which she has to do three *ghusls* in the day for her daily prayers.

The feeling of extraordinary burden would only apply during profuse bleeding. And in this case, if she finds it to be unbearable, then she can do *tayammum* instead of *ghusl* on a case-by-case basis.

# 4. Pre-Natal Bleeding

As mentioned in part one, it is possible for a pregnant woman to have menstruation. In this section we shall discuss the nature of any blood seen during a pregnancy.

Salmān al-Fārsī asked Imām 'Alī (a.s.) about the sustenance of a child in a mother's womb. The Imām said, "Almighty Allāh preserves the (blood of) menstruation for him and turns it into his sustenance in his mother's womb." Sulaymān bin Khālid asked Imām Ja'far aṣ-Ṣādiq (a.s.), "Does a pregnant woman have her monthly period sometimes?" The Imām said, "Yes; and that is because the food of a child in the womb of its mother is the blood. Sometimes the blood is in abundance and is in excess (to his need); and when it is in excess, it is shed out; and when it is shed out (she is regarded as a *ḥã'iz* and) she is not allowed to perform ṣalãt."[1]

* * * * *

If a pregnant woman sees blood and she is **sure** that it is the menstrual flow, then she should consider it as menstruation.

* * * * *

But if she **does not know** whether it is *ḥayz* or *istiḥãza,* then there are four possibilities:

1. If the discharge has all **three signs** of *ḥayz* and it occured during or around the **fixed number** of days, then she should consider it as *ḥayz*.

---

1    Al-'Āmilī, *op. cit.,* vol. 2, p. 579.

2.  If the discharge does **not have all three signs, nor
    did it occur during or around the fixed number**
    of days, then she should consider it as *istiḥāza*.

3.  If the discharge has all **three signs but it did not
    occur during or around the fixed number** of days
    or vice versa, then she should act on precaution
    by performing *wājibat* and refraining from the
    prohibitions.

4.  If the discharge does **not have all three signs,** and
    it occured during or around the **fixed number** of
    days, then she should consider it as *ḥayz*.

*****

If a pregnant woman sees blood **a few days before**
childbirth, then there are four possibilities:

1.  If the bleeding continues up to childbirth, and **she
    knows** that it is menstruation, and it has all three
    signs, then it will be regarded as menstruation.

2.  If the bleeding continues up to childbirth but **she is
    unsure** that it is menstruation – then if it has all three
    signs, or it occurred during the fixed time of her
    menses, it is *ḥayz*; otherwise it will be considered
    as *istiḥāza*.

3.  If the bleeding stopped **ten days before** childbirth
    – then, if it had all three signs, it will be regarded as
    menstruation; otherwise it was *istiḥāza*. In the first
    case, she doesn't have to perform *qazā* of *ṣalāt*; but
    in the second case, she has to perform *qazā* (if she
    had not done the prayers).

4. If the bleeding stopped **during the ten days** prior to childbirth – then, if it had all three signs, or it occurred during the fixed time, it will be regarded as menstruation; otherwise it will be considered as *istiḥāza*. In the first case, she doesn't have to perform *qazã* of *ṣalãt*; but in the second case, she has to do the *qazã* (if she had not done her prayers).

# 5. Forbidden Actions During *Nifãs*

The actions which were forbidden to a *ḥã'iz* woman are also forbidden to a *nafsã'*. A brief list is as follows:

**1.** She is forbidden from touching the Qur'ãn.

**2.** Staying in a mosque or placing something inside it is not allowed to her. Passing through a mosque is only allowed if she enters from one door and, without stopping, goes out of another, with the exceptions of the Sacred Mosque of Mecca and the Prophet's Mosque in Medina, where she cannot even pass through at all. Also remember the difference between a mosque and an *imãmbãrgah* discussed in previous sections.

**3.** She cannot recite the verses of *sajdah*. (See the section on *ḥayz* for more details.)

**4.** Sexual intercourse is forbidden.

**5.** She is excused from *ṣalãt*. Like a *ḥã'iz,* she is not even required to perform them as *qazã*.

**6.** She is also exempted from fasting, but in this case she has to fast afterwards as *qazã*.

See the previous section of the book on 'Actions Forbidden for the *ḥã'iz*' for a more detailed list and explanation.

# 6. *Ghuslu 'n-Nifās*

When *nifās* has ended for a woman, it is *wājib* for her to perform the major ablution. Apart from sexual intercourse, all the acts forbidden to her will remain so until she performs *ghuslu 'n-nifās*.

The manner of performing *ghuslu 'n-nifās* is the same as explained in part one of this book.

* * * * *

# 7. Birth Rituals for a Newborn

Although birth rituals are not part of the *nifās*-related issues, they have been added here for the ease of new parents who seek guidance on the subject. It is recommended to do the following:

1.  **Wash the baby**, provided washing is not harmful to it. Remember, it is not a *ghusl*; it is just a matter of washing the child, *ghaslu 'l-mawlūd*.

2.  Recite the **adhān** in the right ear & the **iqāmah** in the left ear.

3.  Chew a **date** mixed with the water of the Furāt, and *turbat* of Imam Ḥusayn (a.s.). Then rub your clean finger in the mixture and touch the wet finger to the palate (roof of the mouth) of the child.

4.  Provide the child with a **good Muslim name**.

5.  Perform the **aqīqah** on the 7th day after birth. If it is not done on the 7th day, then it can be done later on.

It involves shaving the hair off the head of the baby, as well as giving charity. The charity amount should be equal to the value of silver that is equal to the weight of the cut hair. This charity should be given to the poor and needy and for other areas of charity. Remember that this is a recommendation, not an obligation. So if it is not affordable, it can be skipped or given later on.

**6. Sacrifice** (or arrange to have sacrified) a goat or a sheep or a camel on the 7th day, with the *aqīqah* or without the *aqīqah*. It recommended that the animal chosen for *aqīqah* be healthy, without any physical defects. If it is a goat or sheep, it should preferably  be older than two years of age.

The sacrificial meat may be divided in three parts: one for the poor, one for mu'mineen, and one for relatives. It can be given in the form of raw meat, or a cooked meal. It is strongly discouraged for the parents to eat from that meat.

If this sacrifice was not done by the parents, then it is recommended for the child to do so upon becoming an adult.

Like *aqīqah*, this can be done later if it is not possible on the 7th day.

**7.** Hold a **walīmah** dinner upon the birth of a child, preferably for three days. It means serving food to the relatives and the mu'mineen.

**8.** On the 7th day, have a **circumcision** of the male child done. Circumcision for a male child is *wājib*; and if the parents do not get their son circumcized, then it is *wājib* on the child himself to get circumcised after reaching the age of maturity. It is worth knowing that the validity of the *ṭawāf* of *ḥajj* and *'umrah* of a male pilgrim depends on him being circumcised. However his other rituals, such as *ṣalāt* and those of *ḥajj* and *'umrah*, would still be valid.

The person doing the circumcision of a Muslim child does not need to be a Muslim.

* * *

**Question:** Is **breastfeeding** your child *wājib*?
**Answer:** Breastfeeding your child is highly recommended but not *wājib*.

**Question:** Can I tend to my baby during my *ṣalāt*?
**Answer:** Yes, bending over to pick up your baby, carrying the baby, or feeding the baby during *ṣalāt* does not harm the prayer.

**Question:** Can I **nurse** my baby if I am **in the state of *janābah***? Or will that have spiritual consequences on my baby?
**Answer:** There is no problem in nursing your baby in the state of *janābah*; and there will be no negative consequences on the baby in doing so. If possible, you may perform *wuzū'* before feeding.

**Question:** Are you expected to **fast** what you missed **during pregnancy and during nursing** before the next month of Ramadhān? Or can you pay the *kaffara* and then pay back the fasts when you get a chance?
**Answer:** The fasts missed during pregnancy and breastfeeding have to be done later on. Moreover, you have to pay *fidya* for each missed day. This is different from *kaffara*.

If fasting becomes *wājib* upon you again, and

you did not make up the missed fasts before the next Ramadhãn comes, then you will have to add one more *fidya* for each day missed. For more on *fidya*, see my *Fasting in Ramadhãn: A Simple Guide* at al-m.ca/ramadhan

* * * * *

# <u>Part Four</u>
# <u>Frequently Asked Questions</u>

## *Ḥayz*

**Question 1:** Usually after the continuous bleeding has stopped we will see some slimy light red discharge. In this case, when is the **end of *ḥayz*?** Do we wait until even that clears up before doing *ghuslu 'l-ḥayz?*

**Answer:** In the case of a woman who has a regular pattern, she will follow her regular pattern, e.g., 7 days. If she does not have a regular pattern, and if it comes with all three signs (see the relevant section in the book) all together, then it is to be considered as *ḥayz* for ten days. Any bleeding after ten days is considered as *istiḥāza.*

**Question 2:** I have type 1 **diabetes**. I have a device attached to my body which continuously monitors glucose. I have to replace the devices periodically. Sometimes every 3 days, sometimes every 6 days. I'm also over 40 years of age and have hypothyroidism. My menstrual **cycle fluctuates** and often it happens twice a month. Sometimes it lasts longer than 10 days in which case I have sometimes light, sometimes medium, *istiḥāza.* It is very difficult to change both devices for all the *wājib ghusls.* Moreover it takes 2 hours to calibrate it and that affects my overnight blood sugar levels. Can I do *tayammum* instead of *wãjib ghusl* sometimes?

**Answer:** If it reaches to a level that becomes unbearably difficult (as in your case), then yes, you can do *tayammum* in place of *ghusl*. *Wuzū'* has to be done normally.

**Question 3:** Can we **touch** or hold a *tãboot/'alam* while in the state of a period? What about the Imams' names on these items? Can we visit the shrines?

**Answer:** Touching or holding *tãboot/'alam* is not a forbidden act. However, on the basis of precaution, touching the names of the Imams is forbidden, as is entering the shrines of the Ma'sūmīn. See the section "The Things Forbidden to the *Ḥã'iz*" for more information.

**Question 4: Implantation bleeding** during early pregnancy may occur as spotting or light bleeding over 3 or more days. What would be the ruling?

**Answer:** If it occurs during the monthly cycle time for more than 3 days, then it is *ḥayz*. If it occurs outside the cycle's time or less than 3 days, then it is *istiḥãza*.

**Question 5:** My understanding is that it is not allowed for a woman to insert anything inside her vagina. Does that mean **tampons** worn during periods are *harãm*?

**Answer:** Wearing tampons during a period is permissible. What is forbidden is to use devices for sexual purposes, even if used with one's spouse.

**Question 6:** Do we need to wait until our periods are over to apply **henna** on our hands or hair? If we do apply it during *ḥayz* then does that mean we are najis until the colour wears off?

**Answer:** Henna on your hands or hair is not considered a barrier in doing *wuzū'* or *ghusl*, and so you have to do the *ghusl* as soon as your *ḥayz* ends. It does not effect *najāsat*.

**Question 7:** If a woman finds out that her periods have increased from 7 days to more than 10 days because of a **polyp or cyst** which was discovered after a scan, then should she do *ghuslu 'l-ḥayz* after 7 days and start praying despite the blood?

**Answer:** Since her regular pattern is of 7 days, that will be considered as *ḥayz* and the extra days of bleeding will be considered as *istiḥāza*.

**Question 8:** I have been told that **cyst development** in the ovaries that do not dissolve tend to irregulate the menstruation system. So at times after a regular menstruation cycle, you appear to have bleeding just like menstruation only after two weeks and then the following menstruation comes normally 29 days after the abnormal bleeding event. Your body goes back to a normal schedule and then it happens again after several months again. Do I treat these events as regular menstruation events?

**Answer:** In this case, both bleedings are considered as two separate *ḥayz*.

**Question 9:** During *ḥajj*, sometimes women are asked to follow strict rules regarding *tahārat* during *tawāf* and *sa'ī*. I was once asked to check my sanitary napkin to ensure it was clean before starting *tawāf* and *sa'ī* as I was spotting irregularly. I could only check before leaving my hotel. There was absolutely no way to have checked just before *ṭawāf* and *sa'ī* in the throngs of people. What is the solution for this?

**Answer:** A lady does not have to check herself just before the *ṭawāf* or *sa'ī* as it is not practical; yes, she may check herself before leaving her hotel if there is a spotting concern, and that will be considered enough precaution.

## *Ghusl*

**Question 10:** During *ghusl*, if someone **passes gas or is not sure if they did,** is it necessary to start the *ghusl* all over again? Or can I perform *wuzū'* after completing the *ghusl* and there is no need to start again?

**Answer:** If something that invalidates the *wuzū'* (e.g., passing gas or urinating) happens during the *ghusl*, then she can continue with *ghusl* and it will be valid, but then she has to do *wuzū'* for her prayer.

And if she decides to restart the *ghusl*, then doing the *wuzū'* for her prayer is recommended.

**Question 11:** If a husband and wife have foreplay and the husband **ejaculates** outside of the vagina (no penetration). Is this allowed? Is the wife required to do *ghuslu 'l-janābah*?

**Answer:** There is no problem in what happened. The *ghuslu 'l-janābah* becomes *wājib* on the husband only. As for the wife, it is *wājib* on her only if she had an orgasm (discharge with sexual passion *and* feeling of relaxation).

**Question 12:** Will *ghuslu 'l-janābah* become *wājib* on a woman who has orgasms without penetration and without ejaculation? (For example, by masturbation, dream of a sexual nature, or by manual/oral stimulation by her husband.)

**Answer:** If she has a discharge with sexual passion and feeling of relaxation, then *ghuslu 'l-janãbah* will become *wãjib* on her, even without penetration or ejaculation. (However beware that masturbation in the meaning of self-stimulation is not permissible.) For more, see my book *Marriage & Morals in Islam*.

**Question 13:** If a woman has oral sex rather than vaginal sex with her husband, does she need to do *ghusl* afterwards given that there was no penetration?

**Answer:** Same as above.

**Question 14:** During sexual intercourse, if there is only penetration and no ejaculation, does the woman have to do *ghusl 'l-janãbah*?

**Answer:** Once penetration takes place (even without ejaculation), then both husband and wife become *junub*, and *ghusl 'l-janãbah* becomes *wãjib* on them.

**Question 15:** Is a woman's **discharge** seen after intercourse *najis* (next day or after few hours)?

**Answer:** If the discharge is from the remnant of the discharge of intercourse, then it is *najis*. And if she had already done the *ghusl*, then her *ghusl* would be valid and she has just to wash her private part normally.

**Question 16:** Is *ghusl wãjib* after medical tests? Such as a **pap test**, internal (transvaginal) ultrasound, implanting the IUD and other internal exams done by a doctor.

**Answer:** *Ghusl* does not become *wãjib* for any of these medical tests, nor does it affect the fast of the lady at that time.

## *Miscellaneous*

**Question 17:** Sometimes after doing *wuzū'* we will have a **feeling of gas or bubbles** coming from the area of urination. Does that void the *wuzū'*?

**Answer:** It does not void the *wuzū'*.

**Question 18:** If a lady who goes through a necessary surgery for the **removal of the uterus** has bleeding afterwards, can she pray?

**Answer:** *Ḥayz* comes from the uterus, and so in this case, the bleeding is a result of the surgery which is neither *ḥayz* nor *istiḥāza*. And so she would do the prayer & fast normally.

**Question 19:** When do the *baligha* girls have to start **shaving/removing hair** from their underarms and private parts?

**Answer:** Getting rid of bodily hair (underarms and under the navel) for girls is recommended once every 20 days, but it is not *wājib*. There is no specific age as growth of hair varies between girls. Before marriage, it is better to trim the hair; however, after marriage, using wax or something similar is preferred over shaving.

**Question 20:** Is it okay for a man and a woman to be completely naked during sexual intercourse?

**Answer:** There is no problem in it.

**Question 21:** Is it allowed to get a bikini wax done by a woman?

**Answer:** A woman cannot totally expose her private parts to another woman unless for a medical reason. So she must wear a bikini in this case.

*****

# <u>Monthly Cycle Tracker</u>

**Tracker Key**
Start by creating your tracker key. For Example:

    Spotting
    Light Bleed
    Medium Bleed
    Heavy Bleed

**Date grid**
Then keep track by colouring in the date box each month, this way you will get a visual overview of your periods.

**Cycle length**
Start counting on the first day of your period. The day before your next period is the last day of your menstrual cycle. That's when you stop counting. That's how many days you had in your menstrual cycle that month.

More copies of the calender, and other resources, can be found at https://al-m.ca/nisa.

# Monthly Cycle Tracker

| | 1 | 2 | 3 | 4 | 5 | 6 | 7 | 8 | 9 | 10 | 11 | 12 | 13 | 14 | 15 | 16 | 17 | 18 | 19 | 20 | 21 | 22 | 23 | 24 | 25 | 26 | 27 | 28 | 29 | 30 | 31 |
|---|---|---|---|---|---|---|---|---|---|---|---|---|---|---|---|---|---|---|---|---|---|---|---|---|---|---|---|---|---|---|---|
| Jan | | | | | | | | | | | | | | | | | | | | | | | | | | | | | | | |
| Feb | | | | | | | | | | | | | | | | | | | | | | | | | | | | | | | |
| Mar | | | | | | | | | | | | | | | | | | | | | | | | | | | | | | | |
| Apr | | | | | | | | | | | | | | | | | | | | | | | | | | | | | | | |
| May | | | | | | | | | | | | | | | | | | | | | | | | | | | | | | | |
| Jun | | | | | | | | | | | | | | | | | | | | | | | | | | | | | | | |
| Jul | | | | | | | | | | | | | | | | | | | | | | | | | | | | | | | |
| Aug | | | | | | | | | | | | | | | | | | | | | | | | | | | | | | | |
| Sept | | | | | | | | | | | | | | | | | | | | | | | | | | | | | | | |
| Oct | | | | | | | | | | | | | | | | | | | | | | | | | | | | | | | |
| Nov | | | | | | | | | | | | | | | | | | | | | | | | | | | | | | | |
| Dec | | | | | | | | | | | | | | | | | | | | | | | | | | | | | | | |

**Tracker Key**

| Spotting | Light Bleed | Medium Bleed | Heavy Bleed |
|---|---|---|---|
| | | | |

**Cycle Length**

| Jan | Feb | Mar | Apr | May | Jun | Jul | Aug | Sept | Oct | Nov | Dec |
|---|---|---|---|---|---|---|---|---|---|---|---|
| | | | | | | | | | | | |